The Puzzle of Instruction

SOCIAL-EMOTIONAL LEARNING INTEGRATION IN ALL CONTENT AREAS

Kasia Gutierrez & Christa Pruss

Principal Principles Publications
United States of America

Copyright © 2023 by Gutierrez & Pruss.

All rights reserved. No part of this publication may be reproduced, distributed, or transmitted in any form or by any means, including photocopying, recording, or other electronic or mechanical methods, without the prior written permission of the publisher, except in the case of brief quotations embodied in critical reviews and certain other noncommercial uses permitted by copyright law. For permission requests, write to the publisher, addressed "Attention: Permissions Coordinator," at the address below.

Gutierrez & Pruss
www.confidencecoaches4kids.org.
confidencecoaches4kids@gmail.com

Book Layout ©2017 BookDesignTemplates.com

Ordering Information:
Quantity sales. Special discounts are available on quantity purchases by corporations, associations, and others. For details, contact the "Special Sales Department" at the address above.

Book Title/ Author Name. —1st ed.
ISBN 978-1-7346374-8-9

TABLE OF CONTENTS

- DEDICATION 3
- **INTRODUCTION** 5
- **HOW DOES THIS WORK?** 19
  - LOOKING AT THE BIG PICTURE 20
  - GETTING ORGANIZED: PLANNING AND 21
  - PREPARATION 21
  - BUILDING THE PUZZLE 22
  - PLACING THE LAST PIECE 23
- **SELF-AWARENESS** 27
  - GETTING ORGANIZED 32
  - QUESTIONING PROMPTS TO GET STARTED WITH SELF-AWARENESS INTEGRATION 34
  - BUILDING THE PUZZLE 36
  - COACHING PROMPTS FOR SELF-AWARENESS 42
  - REFLECTION AND SHARING 42
  - SAMPLE SEL PLANNER FOR SELF-AWARENESS 45
  - PLACING THE LAST PIECE 46
  - EDUCATOR SELF-AWARENESS JOURNAL 48
  - REFLECTIONS 48
- **SELF-MANAGEMENT** 53
  - GETTING ORGANIZED 56
  - BUILDING THE PUZZLE 59
  - ORGANIZATIONAL TIPS AND TRICKS 64
  - SAMPLE SEL PLANNER FOR SELF-MANAGEMENT 68
  - PLACING THE LAST PIECE 69
  - EDUCATOR SELF-MANAGEMENT 72

JOURNAL REFLECTIONS 72

SOCIAL-AWARENESS 77
GETTING ORGANIZED 82
BUILDING THE PUZZLE 84
SAMPLE SEL PLANNER FOR SOCIAL AWARENESS 92
PLACING THE LAST PIECE 93
EDUCATOR SOCIAL AWARENESS JOURNAL REFLECTIONS 97

RELATIONSHIP SKILLS 101
GETTING ORGANIZED 105
BUILDING THE PUZZLE 107
SAMPLE SEL PLANNER FOR RELATIONSHIP SKILLS 114
PLACING THE LAST PIECE 115
EDUCATOR RELATIONSHIP SKILLS 117
JOURNAL REFLECTIONS 117

DECISION-MAKING SKILLS 121
GETTING ORGANIZED 125
BUILDING THE PUZZLE 128
SAMPLE SEL PLANNER FOR 135
RESPONSIBLE DECISION-MAKING 135
PLACING THE LAST PIECE 136
EDUCATOR RESPONSIBLE DECISION-MAKING 138
JOURNAL REFLECTIONS: 138

CONCLUSION 143
ADMIRING THE FINISHED PUZZLE 144

DEDICATION

We dedicate this book to the many exhausted educators out there, still showing up each day, teaching from their hearts:

To the educator that takes the time to know their students, to make them feel seen, heard, and valued.
To the educator that takes time to reflect, grow, and continue to learn.
To the educator that takes time to recharge.
To the educator that spends time communicating with families.
To the educator that builds relationships, which in turn impacts the overall success of students' learning and growth.
To the educator that weaves in social emotional learning because it's who they are; not something they have to do.
To the educator that builds emotional safety and supports perseverance for risks and challenges.

In addition, we thank our families for their love and support of our work and dreams. Jay, Nate, Isabelle, Jackson, Katelyn, Carter, and Jeffrey, we couldn't do any of this without you all. To our parents, for always celebrating with us when we FaceTime early in the morning with positive news.

INTRODUCTION

Academic standards and content—that's our responsibility as teachers, right?! If you've been in education for any length of time, you understand this is just one aspect of our role. We've always known there's much more to our job than instruction. If you spend a day in a classroom, you'll likely see teachers supporting kids as a counselor, behavior specialist, and sometimes as a backup parent. We understood this before 2020, but it took navigating the Covid-19 pandemic to clearly see the depth of student needs. As experienced educators, we are struggling more than ever, and we know we are not alone. We've been challenged and pushed to our limits, as we stand in the gap for our students, attempting to teach to the whole child. Now, it feels that the gap is as large as the Grand Canyon. During the "good" moments, we know we are growing as educators, yet we remain feeling defeated and overwhelmed. We are experiencing what Marc Bracket, the author of Permission to Feel calls "emotional labor." Our roles and responsibilities within our classrooms and schools have constrained our ability to express the emotions we are feeling. This has led to burnout, dissatisfaction, and a state of high cortisol levels throughout our days. It's no wonder we are hanging in our staff rooms, eating every sugary or salty snack in sight. We are seeking some relief! Then you layer these uncomfortable emotions with our students' experiences navigating a pandemic. They have lagging skills around emotional regulation, self-management, and stamina for learning. Educators are struggling like never before.

We hear the buzz around the importance of self-care for ourselves and social-emotional learning for our students, but what does that mean exactly? It would be lovely to intentionally practice mindfulness during the day or remember to take a walk during lunch. The reality is, we hit the ground running from the time our alarms go off until we fall into bed, exhausted each night. In addition, how do we teach social-emotional learning when there is so much academic content, while also taking care of ourselves? If we are focused on "accelerating learning," how can we fit it all in? As Confidence Coaches for Kids, we've spent the last several years intentionally focusing on the social emotional needs of students, without knowing how it would also benefit our own mental health and wellness. We believe it's possible to support students' needs without giving up instructional time or falling drastically behind on a pacing guide. More importantly, when you do this successfully, you create a healthy community with opportunities to support your own need for self-care and wellness. We're not saying it will be easy, but nothing worth doing is typically easy or quick. It will, however, make a difference for both you as the educator and the students you serve.

What do you love about teaching? What keeps you motivated in the classroom each day? For us, it has always been about the kids. Although we love to teach engaging content, we get our energy from interaction with students. Specifically, we love to coach them as they push themselves to grow, while in turn, they encourage us to push ourselves to grow. We are there to support them when they fall and to cheer them on as they soar, and they tend to do the same for us. To truly understand our hearts for kids, we should start by sharing how our journey of connecting content to social and emotional learning began.

We were 6th grade teachers, and at the time, our students were placed into leveled math classes. While we were using the same curriculum, one of us taught students performing on grade level, while the other taught students working below grade-level standards. Another teammate taught "accelerated" students, working above grade level. To be honest, we already knew that ability grouping students was not best practice. The research was clear that it was detrimental for kids' learning. However, grouping by ability at our school was what was "traditionally" done. The parent community expected it, and the kids came to 6th grade excited to be in the "high" math class, or embarrassed and ashamed to be in the "low" class. How many times as educators do we just do what we've always done? Why do we ignore our gut and continue with the status quo when we know it isn't right? At some point, you get sick and tired of doing what you know isn't working, and you finally stand up for what you know is right. This wouldn't have been possible if we weren't focused on our students' perspective and ready to grow in our belief in our own self-efficacy.

From the beginning of the year, it wasn't working for us or our students. We were struggling to engage them in mathematical discourse, and they avoided taking risks around their thinking, like the plague. The students were miserable, and so were we. They weren't taking risks, so we were less likely to take risks with our instruction. We felt defeated and unmotivated, almost dreading the math block, which began to affect our lives outside of school. We've never been the teachers who just push through content, and we knew something had to change. Around the same time, we were given the opportunity to take a course titled "Implementing Mathematical Reform." Not only would it help us with our practice, but it was also hosted at our district office and covered by our school district. We were in! Over the eight weeks of the course, we were pushed outside our comfort zone. So much so, that we seriously thought of quitting the class and going back to our old habits. The class was highly influenced by the work of Jo Boaler, from Stanford University. She challenged traditional philosophy around math instruction, proving that ALL students can be mathematicians. We studied our math curriculum inside and out and learned high-leverage and culturally responsive instructional strategies that supported engagement and discourse. We couldn't go back to what we were doing, and we had to make a change.

Have you ever had an experience when you were about to pitch an idea, knowing you would be looked at like you were completely crazy? Well, that's exactly what we faced when we met with our principal at the time, Sarah Crane. At a time when teachers and parents were screaming from the rooftops about high-class sizes, we asked to combine our two math classes into one. We shared what we had learned about growth mindset, brain research, high-leverage tasks, and instructional practices. For many of us, having an accountability partner makes stepping out of our comfort zones less scary. We wanted to take risks within our own teaching, and having each other would give us the courage to try new things to support kids. Thankfully, Sarah believed in us and gave us the go-ahead. Looking back now, as a current building administrator (Kasia), I can only imagine the pushback she initially got from parents and district administrators. If she did get complaints, she never let on. She must have trusted us more than we trusted ourselves, because from that day on, we stuffed 55 sixth graders into a stinky, dilapidated portable from the 90s, every day for math.

What does this have to do with integrating social-emotional learning? Everything! Math was not the obstacle. Students' mindsets, and our own, were the obstacles. It became clear right away that our students, whether on grade level or behind, struggled to adopt a positive math identity. You know the quote, "Comparison is the thief of joy." Well, comparison was exactly what was getting in the way of our students. Being placed in leveled math classes, and knowing they weren't in the accelerated one, was impacting student learning and performance dramatically. Most students didn't believe in their skills or their potential. If they didn't know the answer, they were not going to participate. (Sometimes, even if they did know the answer, they didn't speak up. The possibility of shame at providing the wrong answer was too big a risk.) This had to change because it was impacting their potential to grow. We backed up. We began with Jo Boaler's YouCubed Week of Inspirational Math. This helped us to teach our students, and to learn more ourselves, about the brain and how learning works. It provided us with math tasks that supported math explanations in visuals, numbers, and words. For the first time, we were clear on how to provide different entry points for mathematics based on students' knowledge. The most important thing that changed was our questioning. No longer would our students be off the hook with just providing an answer. They would tell us how and why they thought the way they did. We would push students to explain each other's thinking in their own words or to provide a visual representation. Eventually, little by little, our students were vulnerable enough to actually say, "I'm not sure if my answer is right, but I'll give it a shot." It was music to a math teacher's ears!

We were unprepared to see how changing our questioning and prompting would impact our students' willingness to engage in math. Through consistent high expectations and coaching around discourse, they began to come out of their shells and truly engage in math class. This led to our increased engagement too! We began to look forward to the math block all day, and we couldn't wait to share our experience with our colleagues and families. The truth is, after a certain number of years of teaching, things can feel predictable and stale. This was the experience that revitalized us and helped us fall back in love with teaching.

We heard someone once say, "Our students won't think right if they don't feel right," and we couldn't agree more. Students will not access content if their minds and hearts are worrying about other things. Unfortunately, there will always be worries, but strategic questioning allows us to connect with students while supporting their social and emotional needs. We can provide the instruction needed for students to move forward in their educational careers. There is no doubt academic instruction is important, but can we also take a minute to think about the skills we use today in our own professional lives? Do you use ALL the skills that you learned in school at your place of work? We must think about the big picture for our students. We want them to be career, college, and community ready. To be able to understand themselves and others, they need to know how to think critically, problem-solve, and communicate. As educators, we can develop these skills by providing learning opportunities that integrate social and emotional competencies. Reading, writing, math, science, and social studies are essential and need to be taught in schools; however, we believe our students are not going to digest or retain the content if they have lagging social and emotional skills.

We stand behind our view that relationships lead to rigor, and we would argue that integrating social and emotional learning supports relationships with students. There is no need to change WHAT you teach, but we would like you to consider adjusting HOW you teach. What led you to this profession? Was it kids? Was it a passion for a specific content area? Was it the perceived work-life balance? For most of us, we didn't expect that teaching kids would involve so much more than just academics. As teachers, we are also counselors, coaches, and mental health coordinators, while dabbling in behavior specialist work. How many hats can one person wear? We already have full plates, AND something needs to change. We are not suggesting that you need to add one more thing; instead, just provide the necessary tweaks for you and your students to thrive. Social-emotional learning can't just be a box that gets checked off each day during your morning meeting or advisory class. As educators, we are already doing many wonderful things in our classrooms and schools that support our students in these areas, but it's time to make these areas an authentic and intentional part of each subject area.

We are not just coaches of kids, but we are also teacher coaches in the area of classroom climate and culture. Teachers have the true power to change the outcome for our students, by supporting the whole child, not just academics. Throughout this book, there are explanations of CASEL's (Collaborative for Academic Social and Emotional Learning) 5 social-emotional competencies: self-awareness, self-management, social awareness, relationship skills, and responsible decision-making. We will connect them to common core standards and explain how to integrate the competencies with academic instruction. We will make clear connections regarding how the competencies align with culturally responsive teaching practices, ensuring our students are prepared for life beyond our PreK–12 system. Even more impactful is the reflection we will ask you to do around understanding your OWN social and emotional skills. Being leaders in this work calls for us to walk alongside our students as we grow in our own journey. For each section, you will find personal ideas and journal prompts to go deeper in your understanding of yourself.

You may be thinking, "I'm a math teacher. What do these social-emotional skills have to do with math?" or "Isn't this an elementary thing?" There's a misconception that teaching social and emotional skills is something only elementary teachers do. Or, that it should be regulated to the 20 minutes of advisory, or maybe a counselor's guidance lesson. Not true. "SEL improves academic achievement by an average of 11 percent, increases appropriate social behavior, improves students' attitudes, and reduces depression and stress" (Durlak, Weissberg, Dymnicki, Taylor & Schellinger, 2011). As your climate and culture coaches, we will inspire you to integrate standards through a social, emotional, and safety lens, for the benefit of you and your students. Wouldn't you love to plan a math lesson in which students didn't shut down or leave the room? How would it feel to engage your students in a Socratic seminar discussion where celebrating different perspectives was not only encouraged but welcomed? Can students pause to consider the impact before making a decision that affects their collaborative learning group? When taught with intention, our students can do anything.

If you are still unsure about this whole social-emotional learning integration thing, we have some questions for you.

1. How's it going for you as a teacher right now?
2. Do your students come to school each day ready to learn?
3. Are they emotionally regulated and consistently making good decisions?
4. Do they understand how to prioritize and plan for long-term projects? Does group work typically go well for all students?
5. Are they quick to examine their own biases and consider perspectives other than their own?

If you answered no to any of the questions above, our next question is this: What would it hurt to try something new? You are not alone. You will have us by your side, coaching you on how to put the pieces of the social and emotional learning puzzle together.

Now, let's get started.

SECTION 1

HOW DOES THIS WORK?

We have put together a plan for learning how to integrate academic social and emotional learning (SEL) practices into specific content areas. We have broken the SEL competencies into 4 sections to help explain and realistically model instructional practices and delivery of content. Our ultimate goal for students is to learn "standards and competencies that articulate what students should know and be able to do for academic success, school and civic engagement, health and wellness, and fulfilling careers" as stated well by CASEL. This feels overwhelming and maybe even like one more thing on your full teacher plate. We are here to show you how to tweak and shift your instructional practices, which will ultimately benefit you and your students.

LOOKING AT THE BIG PICTURE

When starting any puzzle, whether it's 100 or 500 pieces, you start by looking at the picture on the front to gain an understanding of the task at hand. Sometimes, the picture on the box feels manageable, while other times it feels daunting. All puzzle boxes provide a visual of the final product. This is where we consider our motivation and willingness to try new strategies to complete the puzzle. To create a clear picture of how the SEL competencies develop and are expressed, each "Looking at the Big Picture" section begins with CASEL's definition. It continues with understanding how the competencies connect to academic subject areas. Consider this section to be your call to action—the importance behind this work and why you need to be integrating this in your classroom, school, and community.

GETTING ORGANIZED: PLANNING AND PREPARATION

Once you have a grasp on the big picture, it's time to get organized. Do you want to start with the edges, colors, or sections of the puzzle? To complete the Puzzle of Instruction, planning, and preparation are key. This section lays out the role of the teacher and student within each competency. Basic questioning prompts are provided to get started with planning and integration of SEL and academics. Use these roles and questions as tools to guide your planning and delivery of instruction. Ask yourself, what should I be doing as a teacher, and in turn, what should I see from my students? A word of caution: be careful not to overwhelm yourself with too many pieces trying to find evidence of yourself and students in the table provided. Set a realistic goal, pick one, and strive to focus on that specific area for you and your students. With time and experience, you can add to your practice.

BUILDING THE PUZZLE

You have a grasp of the big picture and a plan of focus and action. Now it's time to connect those pieces, integrating questioning prompts, standards, lesson plans, and high-leverage strategies. You begin to build engagement and connection for students, and joy and momentum for you as an educator. Through the sample lessons provided, you will clearly see the connection between Social Emotional Learning and academics come together within your practice. It can be difficult to see yourself as more than a math or science teacher, but in this section, let's work to shift your vision of yourself to a coach and an instructor. This will take patience, flexibility, and the willingness to take care of yourself by stepping back and taking a break at times. The completion of this section will provide a sample SEL Planner completed by us, to show you how to bring your lesson to life.

PLACING THE LAST PIECE

The final picture is now in view, and the puzzle is almost finished. You can see it and begin to enjoy and celebrate the hard work you have accomplished. For our students, this picture is their development of skills and life beyond the PreK-12 system. Placing the Last Piece makes the connection between the work you do today in your classroom, to the work the students do when they move on, to build their own puzzles.

How will our coaching of SEL competencies within academic content support our students to be career, college, and community ready? We believe the work we do leads our students to being aware, eligible, and prepared for the world. Our students not only need the academic and technical skills necessary for the workforce, but more importantly, they need opportunities to develop deeper human skills. They need preparation to pursue their career and life goals with interpersonal, communication, critical thinking, and perspective-taking skills to work collaboratively with others. This is the goal, but we can't take for granted that all students come to us with exact needs. SEL without a focus on equity will further create a gap between our white and our traditionally marginalized students. This is where we, as educators, need to prioritize building strong relationships with all students.

> *"It becomes imperative to understand how to build positive social relationships that signal to the brain a sense of physical, psychological, and social safety so that learning is possible." –*
>
> *Zaretta Hammond*

Feeling safe is the key to learning and is supported by brain science. Our question is, do all students GET to feel safe in the traditional school environment? Also, do you GET to feel safe? Standing in the gap for students means ensuring they all feel safe. To do this, we must understand how our students' brains react to the environment we provide. When our students are feeling safe, in their comfort zone, positive relationships are strong and connection with others feel easy. Dopamine and serotonin chemicals are on the rise and the environment feels comfortable. This is a great foundation for student learning, but there is more to learning than just being in our comfort zone. Students have to move into the risk zone, to further grow and learn. When entering the risk zone, another feel-good chemical called oxytocin is released. They become excited and are willing to accept challenges while learning new concepts. This is the sweet spot for learning, or what Vygotsky called the "zone of proximal development." Another zone our students may experience, complete with its own chemical cortisol, is the flight, fight, or freeze zone. This may look like a student shutting down, exhibiting defensiveness, or even endangering themselves or others. This zone not only breaks our hearts to witness, but it's also the zone where learning cannot take place. The truth is, our students are in this zone more often than we realize.

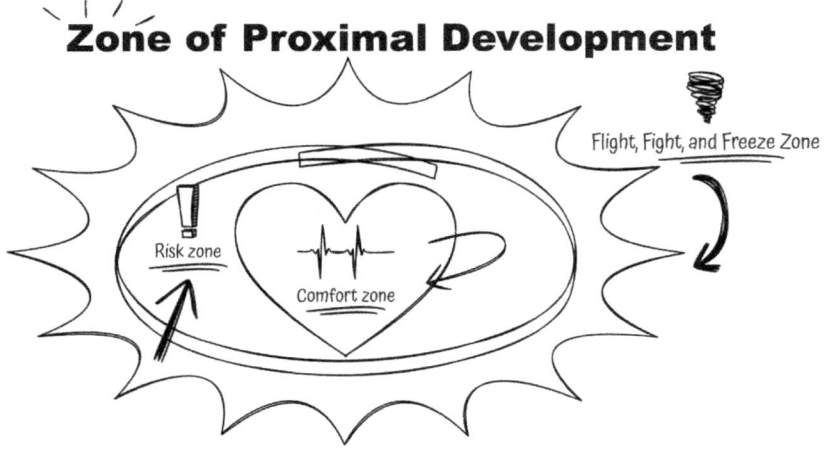

So what do we do? Our students come to us from different backgrounds and cultures, with varying experiences. Their needs differ, and as educators, we must strive to implement equitable practices that meet students where they are. Let's be committed to avoiding the perpetuation of harmful environments we may create, based on our own biases and experiences. The way things have always been done isn't always the best way. We want to ensure all students can pursue their goals and dreams, prepared with whatever they need. Students deserve to learn the skills they need to build their own life puzzles.

SECTION 2

SELF-AWARENESS

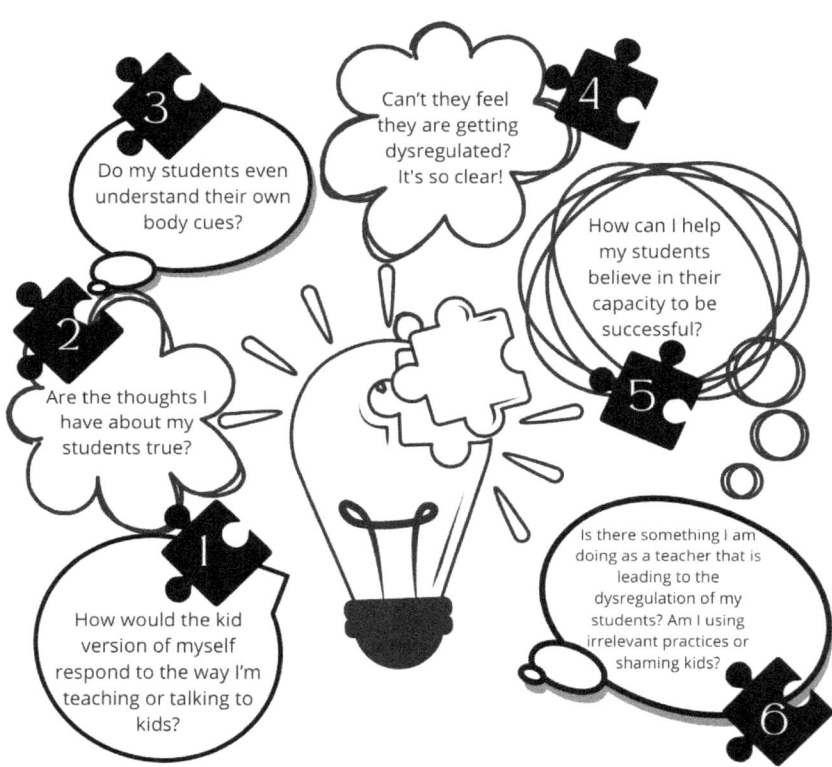

THE PUZZLE OF INSTRUCTION • 29

CASEL Definition of Self-Awareness: The ability to understand one's emotions, thoughts, and values, and how they influence behavior across contexts. This includes the capacity to recognize one's strengths and limitations, with a well-grounded sense of competence and purpose.

- Identify emotions
- Accurate self-perception
- Identify personal and social identities
- Recognize personal, cultural-linguistic assets
- Self-confidence
- Self-efficacy

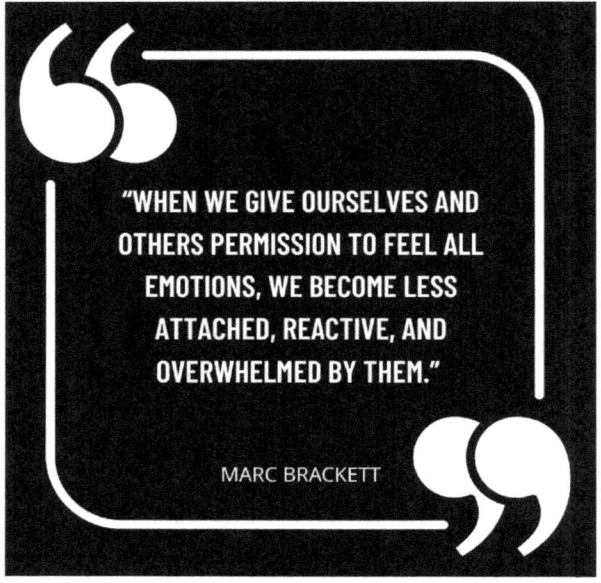

"WHEN WE GIVE OURSELVES AND OTHERS PERMISSION TO FEEL ALL EMOTIONS, WE BECOME LESS ATTACHED, REACTIVE, AND OVERWHELMED BY THEM."

MARC BRACKETT

"Is it really my job to teach my kids to understand themselves? I thought I was a PE teacher." The truth is, we're not just teachers of standards. Let's consider the big picture we have for our students. If we want them to be ready for learning today, and career, college, and community ready after they leave us, they need support in developing self-awareness skills. Without truly knowing themselves—their thoughts, emotions, and reactions—students tend to lack control in their response to situations. They react without thinking, or they get into situations repeatedly that are difficult for them to process or handle. They need to understand their triggers to effectively know themselves. Without these skills, they will not learn in your classroom. When our students are feeling anxious, overwhelmed, nervous, scared, or overly excited, they are unable to access the instruction we provide. Their ability to use their working memory and to apply skills literally shuts down.

As educators, we have two choices: we can get frustrated with our students' lack of learning, OR we can set them up for success by explicitly teaching them HOW to be self-aware, so they can access the content. We communicate to our students that the only thing we can control is our effort, beliefs, and attitude. The same goes for us! If we aren't self-aware, how will we support our students in this skill? It's okay to be vulnerable in front of students and to communicate your thoughts and emotions. Model this for kids, and they will see it is beneficial and normal when emotions and reactions pop up. When we take time to understand ourselves, we are setting ourselves and our students up to be more proactive with managing emotions in class. So how do we do this for our students?

GETTING ORGANIZED

As you begin the journey of supporting self-awareness, it's important to know the roles you as the educator and the students play. Understanding what we already have in place, helps us know what is still needed to put the puzzle together. A tool we developed to support this work is our CASEL Competencies Look-for-Tool. Below, you will see intentional teacher moves that result in positive self-awareness and student outcomes. As you read through the table, start with celebrating what you already do as a teacher and the areas your students consistently demonstrate. After, pick a goal for you and your students to develop during your lessons, units, and throughout the year. Start slow and remember, just like the Tanzanian proverb, "Little by little, a little becomes a lot."

Teacher Moves

Explicitly teach and support student identification of emotions and correlating body cues.

Attempt to understand each student's background, culture, interests, and identity to shape teaching decisions.

Model and support the development of a growth mindset in our students.

Encourage self-reflection in students through modeling self-reflection of strengths and struggles regularly.

Provides opportunities for students to assess their own learning for strengths and opportunities.

Student Moves

Become an emotional detective. Understand and name one's emotions, thoughts, and values.

Develop an awareness of body cues and their connection to emotions and thoughts.

Understand self-talk and its effect on behavior, including a growth or fixed mindset.

Identify strengths and struggles.

WHOA! That's a lot of things to think about in addition to standards and the pacing guide. Worried about where to begin? We've already discussed how a focus on questioning strategies transformed our teaching.

QUESTIONING PROMPTS TO GET STARTED WITH SELF-AWARENESS INTEGRATION

Here are some sample questioning prompts to help students engage in self-awareness, so they can access instructional content:

1 What emotions do you feel during a typical (math/science/ELA) lesson? Overwhelmed? Worried? Excited? Bored? Why do you think these emotions come up for you during this class?

② Do you have a real-world connection to this lesson? Does it remind you of any experiences you have had? How do your connections affect your emotions?

③ Do you believe you can be successful in class? Do you have room to grow as a learner? Which areas are you successful in, and where do you want to improve?

④ What strategies can you use when you are feeling difficult emotions while trying to learn? If you don't know, who can you reach out to for help?

⑤ How are you feeling? How do your feelings impact your learning in this lesson?

⑥ How do you communicate your thoughts and feelings with your table group (both comfortable and uncomfortable)?

BUILDING THE PUZZLE

Self-awareness in math? Yep. Let's first consider where our students are since experiencing the COVID-19 pandemic. How many of our students come in with hoodies up, put their heads down, or completely disengage? OR when was the last time during a lesson a student got frustrated and left...maybe knocking a chair over on their way out? According to recent 2021 research from the Centers for Disease Control and Prevention, "More than a third (37%) of high school students reported they experienced poor mental health during the COVID-19 pandemic, and 44% reported they persistently felt sad or hopeless during the past year." Without trying to sound harsh, it would be irresponsible to ignore this reality as educators, as we attempt to support our students and ourselves. First, consider how we can support our student's ability to identify emotions before they are consumed by them and unable to access instruction.

Here is an example of a typical 6th-grade math standard:

Apply and extend previous understandings of multiplication and division to divide fractions by fractions:

CCSS.MATH.CONTENT.6.NS.A.1 : Interpret and compute quotients of fractions, and solve word problems involving division of fractions by fractions, e.g., by using visual fraction models and equations to represent the problem. For example, create a story context for (2/3) ÷ (3/4) and use a visual fraction model to show the quotient; use the relationship between multiplication and division to explain that (2/3) ÷ (3/4) = 8/9 because 3/4 of 8/9 is 2/3. (In general, (a/b) ÷ (c/d) = ad/bc.) How much chocolate will each person get if 3 people share 1/2 lb of chocolate equally? How many 3/4-cup servings are in 2/3 of a cup of yogurt? How wide is a rectangular strip of land with a length of 3/4 mi and an area of 1/2 square mi?

Confused or overwhelmed by this extensive standard? If you're like us, you had to read it a few times to actually comprehend what it was asking. Now consider your 12-year-old student, just returning from lunch after a fight with a friend over a recent social media post. Is it possible they might not have the stamina or motivation to engage with this standard at this time? Knowing our students don't always come to us with regulated emotions or feeling thrilled to learn, we need to consider HOW we can anticipate areas of instruction that might lead our students down a path toward dysregulation. Which part of this standard can you predict will lead to negative self-talk in your students? Is it wordy? Is there an access point for students with limited previous understanding? Have you ever heard a student say, "I can't do fractions"? We suggest starting with an easily accessible activity to ease students into the task. Following is our approach to begin to build the puzzle with our students.

Math Journal Opening- Start the class with intention. Yes, your class periods are short. Yes, you have A LOT of standards to get through. And, if you miss the opportunity to support your student's development of a positive math identity, you will fight it all year long. Take the first 1-3  minutes to help them get in the right frame of mind for the lesson. Set your emotional intention for this class by allowing students to journal at the beginning of class:

Sample journal prompt: Name and visualize the emotion you want to feel during today's lesson. Is there anything on your mind that could hold you back, or lead to a lack of participation?

Math lesson/practice- Using what you know about your students' mathematical identity and growth vs.

fixed mindset, begin by asking what they think of when they hear the word fraction? Ask them to describe the feeling they have in their body when they see a fraction problem. Does their stomach feel uneasy? Do they get hot or sweaty? Maybe they're excited to solve a problem. Just as we encourage students to address their emotions and possible barriers during the journal prompt, we also help them by prompting them to take time to acknowledge their feelings throughout the lesson. Then discuss how fractions are used in the real world. Why might they need to know how to divide fractions?

If you have never used a compendium (an anchor chart on steroids) to guide your instruction and support your students, now is the time. (See the picture below.) Inquiry is one focus area of a compendium. This is an opportunity for students to share what they think they know, and want to learn, and questions they may have about the concept being taught. If students are uncomfortable with the academic concept, having the opportunity to focus on inquiry helps to calm their emotions so they can access the material and keep their working memory engaged.

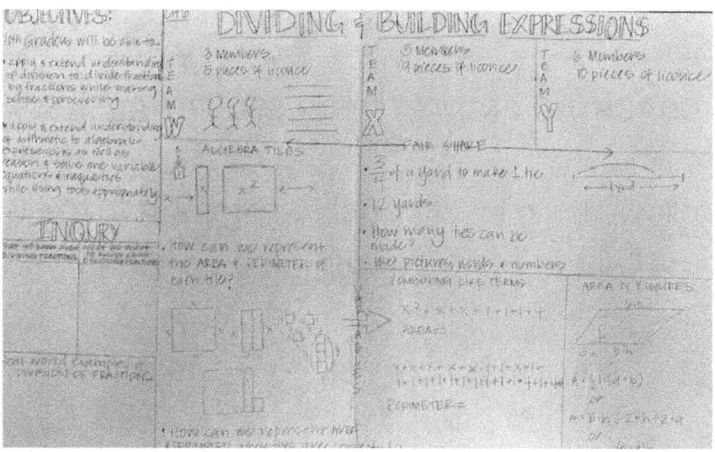

It's important to prompt throughout the lesson for student reflection around self-talk. In particular, our students can struggle with "all or nothing" thinking, with thoughts such as, "I'm the worst at math," or, "This sucks. I'm stupid, and so is my teacher." Also, they will be experiencing emotional body cues that may be uncomfortable. Don't let this opportunity go by! Acknowledge the negative thinking and emotions. More importantly, model think-alouds to combat the negative self-talk and difficult emotions tied to the content. They will not do this on their own. They need our example and coaching to thrive in our classrooms and beyond.

COACHING PROMPTS FOR SELF-AWARENESS

The following is a list of coaching prompts to use when you see your students struggling:

- → Acknowledge body cues. Pay attention to what your body is telling you.
- → Can you name the emotion you think you're having?
- → Take a breath as you feel these sensations. What do you need?
- → Attempt to understand the WHY behind your thinking. Are the thoughts you are thinking always true? If not, why are they coming up now?
- → Consider what you already know and how it can help you.

REFLECTION AND SHARING

Ending class with reflection will allow students the opportunity to self-evaluate their learning and emotions, to guide future learning. Reflection as a daily habit will support students to successfully understand themselves as learners, knowing what they need from themselves, their peers, and their teachers. Academic growth and achievement are sure to follow with such practice. Consider the following questions for students to respond to in their math journals, to guide them through the self-reflection process:

- 💭 What were the body cues you experienced throughout the lesson?
- 💭 Where in the lesson did you catch yourself experiencing negative self-talk or a fixed mindset?
- 💭 Was there a time you felt confident? Was there a time you didn't? Describe.

It's essential to provide time for students to share with a partner or their table group. For some students, verbal sharing is too overwhelming at first. One idea is to have them complete an exit ticket. They could use a sticky note to answer the questions, and turn it in before leaving. Ultimately, we want to understand how students' self-awareness is affecting their ability to access the content. In our math classroom, when students finished reflecting, we took the time for celebration. Students had an opportunity to acknowledge one another for their efforts, mindset, communication, and perseverance. This encouraged a safe learning community, where risk-taking and individual identity were valued.

SAMPLE SEL PLANNER FOR SELF-AWARENESS

Subject: Math   Unit: Fractions   Dates:

Standard/Objective: CCSS.MATH.CONTENT.6.NS.A.1
Interpret and compute quotients of fractions, and solve word problems involving division of fractions by fractions, e.g., by using visual fraction models and equations to represent the problem.

SEL Competency Focus: Students will be able to identify and describe their thoughts and feelings in connection to fraction application.

SEL Objective: I can describe my feelings and thoughts about fractions to help myself persevere and ask questions.

Teacher Moves & Roles:	Student Moves & Roles:	Questions & Coaching Prompts to Consider:
Explicitly teach and support student identification of emotions and correlating body cues.	Develop an awareness of body cues and their connection to emotions and thoughts	• Acknowledge body cues: Pay attention to what your body is telling you. • Can you name the emotion you think you're having? • Consider what you already know and how it can help you.
Model and support the development of a growth mindset in our students.	Understand and name one's emotions, thoughts, and values	

High Leverage Task or Activity: Journaling and Compendium (Inquiry Focus)

Lesson Outline:
Opening:
Journal prompt - Name and visualize the emotion you want to feel during today's lesson. Is there anything on your mind that could hold you back or lead to a lack of participation?

Activity:
What do you know about fractions?
How do fractions make you feel?
What do you want to know about fractions?
How are fractions used in the real world?

Reflection:
What were the body cues you experienced throughout our compendium talk/work today?
Where in the lesson did you catch yourself experiencing negative self-talk or a fixed mindset?
Was there a time today you felt confident? Was there a time you didn't? Which part? Why?

PLACING THE LAST PIECE

While encouraging self-awareness is essential to student success in all content areas, we must think bigger when supporting our students. It's about more than mastering the standards we cover in a year. It's about supporting them to fully understand themselves. In our school district in Oregon, we focus on knowing our students by name, strength, and need. Truly, they must understand these aspects of themselves. Providing practice and reflection around these areas across the school day is how our students will develop true self-awareness. The more they become aware, the more proficient they will be with identifying emotions, developing accurate self-perception, and recognizing their strengths. This leads them on their journey to develop self-efficacy.

Completing the puzzle is rooted in the foundation of self-confidence—the confidence to take risks and step out of their comfort zone. This starts in our classrooms, each time they take the risk to share a personal reflection or emotion. Whether it's a math, reading, or a social studies standard, the classroom climate and culture around self-awareness solidifies our students' willingness to apply these skills. Not just today, but in life beyond their time with us. Employers are seeking a variety of self-awareness skills in their employees, such as positive attitude, flexibility, sense of self-worth, innovation, creativity, and commitment. Just like players on a team, kids need a great self-awareness coach.

The development of self-awareness is an essential skill with long-range benefits. In addition to supporting success in school and beyond, mastering it can prevent barriers around inclusion among peers and marginalization from adults. The thing is, not all students come from backgrounds that support this skill. As educators, the toolbox our students come to us with is out of our control. What's in our control is the environment we provide to support all students thriving.

Providing student self-reflection and self-assessment opportunities allows us to understand how to support our students where they are. However, this is not just valuable for our students; it's valuable for us as educators too. When we provide these opportunities, we gain perspective into our students' backgrounds and the cultural lens they bring into our classrooms. When we understand them, we can intentionally honor their background and emotions, ensuring they grow as learners. As Dr. Dan Siegel said, "You have to name it to tame it." This is essential as we coach our students to move from self-awareness to practicing self-management.

EDUCATOR SELF-AWARENESS JOURNAL REFLECTIONS

The process of self-awareness begins with knowing yourself and your beliefs. Without truly knowing ourselves, our thoughts, our emotions, and our reactions, we tend to lack control over our responses to students.

Understanding yourself is one piece of the puzzle, so get started responding to the following self-awareness prompts on the following page:

EDUCATOR SELF-AWARENESS JOURNAL REFLECTION

How do you handle negative thoughts about students, classes, or your colleagues?

_____
_____
_____
_____
_____
_____
_____
_____

Consider your closest work colleague. How would you respond to their negative thoughts about themselves, students, or colleagues?

_____
_____
_____
_____
_____
_____
_____

Reflect deeper...

_____
_____
_____
_____
_____

Extend my thinking...

STANDING IN THE GAP FOR OUR STUDENTS!

SECTION 3

SELF-MANAGEMENT

THE PUZZLE OF INSTRUCTION • 55

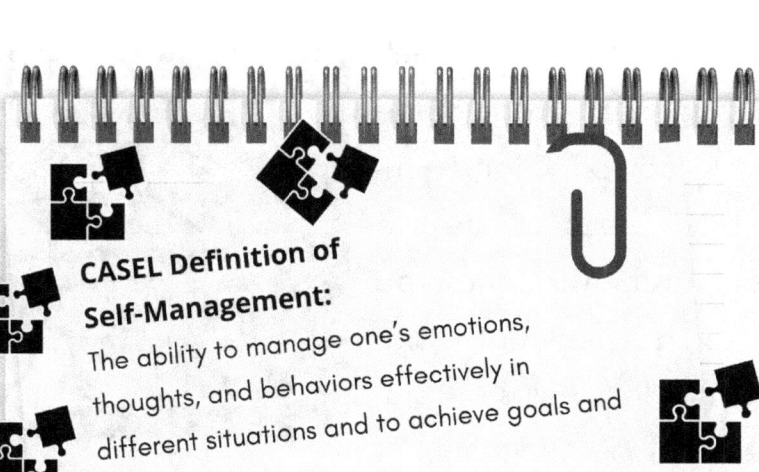

CASEL Definition of Self-Management: The ability to manage one's emotions, thoughts, and behaviors effectively in different situations and to achieve goals and aspirations.

Manage emotions

Stress management strategies

Self-discipline/motivation

Goal setting

Planning and organizing

Courage/agency for self & others

Examine prejudices and biases

Develop interests and sense of purpose

Growth mindset

The ability to practice self-management is one of the most powerful and impactful areas of life we can master. This is the area of social-emotional learning that truly helps our students to be successful in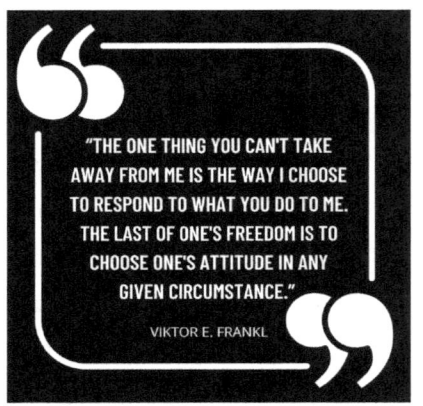
school and life. After developing self-awareness around emotions, strengths, and areas of stress or growth, self-management helps us and our students to step up to attain our goals and self-efficacy.

GETTING ORGANIZED

Just as you did previously with self-awareness, this is your opportunity to celebrate what you and your students already do in the area of self-management. When picking a goal for you and your students, consider what evidence you already see of mastery, and what still needs to be developed.

Teacher Moves

Integrate examples of self-management across all curriculum areas (character examples; emotional regulation in math; opportunities for growth mindset integration)

Support students with a plan of action for both reflection during the assignment and progression to completion (e.g., data binders; reflection exit tickets)

Establish effective routines and expectations to encourage predictability and familiarity

Student Moves

Set an emotion intention; Name and visualize a desired emotion

Actively replace harmful and negative thinking with supportive and positive affirmations (accurate self-perception).

Adopt effective stress management techniques

Identify a safe person and place to process and regulate emotions

Understanding your goals around self-management for your students is the first step, but the truth is, it's difficult at the moment. When teachers or students are feeling dysregulated, it's tough to remain calm. These moments will never become easy, but we will become stronger and more confident in our regulation strategies as we continue to integrate these skills in our practice. It's helpful to have a few key questions in your back pocket when encountering these experiences with students. Here are a few you could try:

> **Questioning Prompts to Get Started with Self-Management Integration**
>
> - What do you need to be successful in completing the assignment?
> - What made you feel proud during the lesson, and how will you incorporate that into future lessons?
> - Your body is showing me you are feeling stressed or frustrated. Is there a strategy that calms your mind and body?
> - What's the plan if your idea fails?
> - How do you continue to practice a skill that is challenging for you?
> - How do you know when you need help? Who do you ask for help when you need it?

BUILDING THE PUZZLE

Self-management has many components that fall under the umbrella of executive function skills. For now, we will focus on the areas of goal setting, planning, and organization. As we continue to acknowledge that our students come to us with different backgrounds, experiences, and identities, we have found that project-based learning benefits all learners, engaging their executive functioning skills.

Standard (Next-Generation Science Standards/ Engineering Design)

MS-ETS1-1. Define the criteria and constraints of a design problem with sufficient precision to ensure a successful solution, taking into account relevant scientific principles and potential impacts on people and the natural environment that may limit possible solutions.

MS-ETS1-2. Evaluate competing design solutions using a systematic process to determine how well they meet the criteria and constraints of the problem.

MS-ETS1-3. Analyze data from tests to determine similarities and differences among several design solutions to identify the best characteristics of each that can be combined into a new solution to better meet the criteria for success.

MS-ETS1-4. Develop a model to generate data for iterative testing and modification of a proposed object, tool, or process such that an optimal design can be achieved.

There are several components that need to be met and mastered in these standards, which can overwhelm our students and even ourselves. First things first, how can you hook them? What can you read, show, or share that will leave the students wanting to explore? We like to provide visuals through the use of videos. For example, Mark Rober's Squirrel Maze is a favorite of students. It clearly illustrates the problem and solution, engages imagination, and supports the research and revision processes needed in engineering and design. Sparking interest in our students facilitates creativity and collaboration while helping to boost their self-motivation for their project.

Our students are now motivated to get started, but they will still need coaching when it comes to backwards planning and time management. While they are "big kids" and think they know how to get their work done and use their time wisely, they are not there yet. Our students need constant reminders, modeling, and coaching on how to set themselves up for success. Organization is an essential skill for success, keeping our students on track to make progress toward their goals. Some may be thinking, "But I'm just not good at organization. I was born without that skill." We get it! I (Kasia) am not organized by nature. However, over the years, I've developed some skills that have ensured I actually keep my job and my little humans alive, while still supporting my students in organization. We do not have to be experts. We need to be willing to walk the talk and own our strengths and weaknesses while modeling how to persevere and work through the struggles.

Supporting organization and planning in our students is further fueled when they feel motivated by having a say in how they demonstrate their learning. Providing choice within engineering and design gives our students a voice; they can choose their project based on interest, accessibility to available resources, or comfort level. Once they decide on their project/experiment, they need to get their student planners ready. Using a rubric can help direct the focus at the beginning with the end in mind. What is the end result they are striving for? What is needed for the project/experiment to be considered complete? Guide the students through each step needing completion before the next and the amount of time required for each step. Using the start and end date to map out the project helps students complete the assignment while also working to maintain organization and avoiding feeling overwhelmed or discouraged.

PROJECT PLANNER

Date	Engineer & Design Process	Ask & Task
	ASK: Identify the need	What is the problem to solve? What do you want to design? Who is it for? What do you want to accomplish? What are the project requirements? What are the limitations? What is your goal?
	Research the problem	Talk to people with different backgrounds and specialties What products and solutions already exist? What technology is needed? What can be adapted?
	Imagine: Develop possible solutions	Brainstorm and collaborate with team Encourage idea (leave judgment behind) Build on ideas as a team Stay on topic
	Plan: Decide on a solution	Consider needs & challenges again Look back at your research Weigh your best choices/options Select your solution Make a plan
	Create: Build your vision	Put your plan into action Continue to consider if it meets the challenges and objectives you set out to solve Push your creativity and imagination
	Test and Evaluate	Does it work? Does it solve the need? Communicate and analyze What needs to be revised? What should stay as is?
	Improve: Revise as needed	How does this improve the problem? Is it a solution? Make revisions Draw new designs Repeat until it is the best it can be

We appreciate the saying, "Failure to plan is planning to fail." In this section, we want to provide some tips and tricks that may help in your student's journey to becoming more organized (and maybe even yours as well).

ORGANIZATIONAL TIPS AND TRICKS

🧩 List making - Where would either of us be without this skill? There is something so satisfying about crossing a finished task off a list. Turns out, your brain actually releases the feel-good chemical dopamine when you scratch something off your list. We love science!

🧩 Visual planners/calendars - Over the years, we've tried many different planners and organizational tools. Until recently, we didn't realize these tools had to be in our line of vision! The saying is "out of sight is out of mind" for a reason. Keep your calendar in a frequently visited area where you're sure to see it daily. We go crazy over color coding and using pretty pens and fonts, but at the very least, you have to remember it to use it.

⁂ Whiteboards - This is connected to the list-making tip above. If you are prone to losing your lists (Kasia), you'll love using a big whiteboard. Students can use them to track their to-do lists and homework assignments all in one VISIBLE place.

⁂ Have a designated place for everything - Have a place for your frequently used items like backpacks, laptops, or school work to save time looking for them. Put your belongings away right away, where they will be when you need them. Seriously, try it for a couple of weeks. You're welcome in advance.

⁂ Timers - We live in a world full of helpful technology, and we love timers. When we're feeling unmotivated to get started, we set a goal for a specific amount of work time. Use your watch, Alexa, or your phone timer, and commit to a short work session. Most times, we find when the timer goes off, we've hit a groove, and we aren't ready to stop working.

Throughout their project, providing encouragement and time for reflection is always wise, as they will feel stuck and overwhelmed during the process. Helping students navigate those feelings as they work towards an end goal will help them persevere during their struggle. Never underestimate the power of a picture book. Even as our students get older, they still enjoy a good read aloud. Analyzing characters from a text opens up the conversation of reflection in a safe way for our students. They are able to speak freely without feeling vulnerable as they critically evaluate the characters' choices. As they do so, they begin to naturally connect themselves to the characters, comparing and contrasting their process. For this project, using specific engineering and design picture books like Rosie Revere, Engineer by Andrea Beaty and The Most Magnificent Thing by Ashley Spires are great resources to use to support reflection and connection to their own projects.

Here are some sample questioning prompts to encourage evaluation by your students:

- What challenges does Rosie face during her design process?
- What challenges have you faced so far?
- How does Rosie handle her challenges?
- What would you do if you were Rosie?
- What should you remember as you begin your build? Why?
- What lesson does the girl learn by the end of the story?

SAMPLE SEL PLANNER FOR SELF-MANAGEMENT

Subject: Science **Unit**: Engineering and Design **Dates**: 3 week project

Standard/Objectives:
Define the criteria and constraints of a design problem with sufficient precision to ensure a successful solution, taking into account relevant scientific principles and potential impacts on people and the natural environment that may limit possible solutions.

Evaluate competing design solutions using a systematic process to determine how well they meet the criteria and constraints of the problem.

Analyze data from tests to determine similarities and differences among several design solutions to identify the best characteristics of each that can be combined into a new solution to better meet the criteria for success.

Develop a model to generate data for iterative testing and modification of a proposed object, tool, or process such that an optimal design can be achieved.

SEL Competency Focus: Managing emotions, thoughts, and behaviors while planning and organizing to reach an end goal.

SEL Objective: I will be able to make a plan to complete my engineering and design project by backwards planning to support my stress management.

Teacher Moves & Roles:	Student Moves & Roles:	Question and Prompts to Consider:
Support students with a plan of action for both reflection during the assignment and progression to completion.	Create a plan involving backwards planning to accomplish goals. Adopt effective stress management techniques.	• What do you need to be successful in completing the assignment? • What's the plan if your idea fails? • How do you know when you need help? Who do you ask for help when you need it?

High Leverage Task or Activity:
Student choice: What is the engineering and design problem you want to solve?

Lesson Outline:
Opening: Mark Rober's Squirrel Maze video

Activity: Backwards planning process and support
Explicit teaching of engineering and design process (detailed guide sheet to break assignment into manageable chunks and due dates).

Reflection/Closing:
Did I meet each of my deadlines?
Did I ask for help when I needed it?
Was I able to remain calm even when I felt overwhelmed?
How could planning support me in other areas?

PLACING THE LAST PIECE

As our students work towards their career, college, and community pathways they continually develop their character as a person throughout their experiences. Self-management practice with regulation strategies, goal setting, and planning provide our students tools they will need to navigate independence and adulthood. Having a plan can help alleviate stress and anxiety. Breaking projects into more manageable chunks and making lists support accomplishment and progress while helping them to see how far they have come in reaching their goals. And, as we mentioned earlier, choice equals voice. Our students will be more invested and motivated when they have a say and ownership in their learning and work.

Regulating emotions and reactions is also a part of this process. As adults, we experience emotions each day and our response and ability to manage them is imperative to our success as professionals. As educators, we have an opportunity to guide our students through managing their reactions and responses to their feelings in a proactive manner. Just like for us, there will always be someone they work with who pushes their buttons, and there will be times of disappointment. Fleeing the classroom, yelling, or becoming physical are strategies that create greater obstacles (and this doesn't just apply to our students). Use these teachable moments to support their ability to walk through uncomfortable feelings and situations so they come out stronger on the other side. The goal is for them to use strategies that help return them to their best self. What can they do to support themselves in those moments? Is it backwards planning, deep breathing, taking a walk, or making a list? Our classrooms should be a safe place for them to practice and learn about themselves. Their original plan may end with a different outcome, creating an opportunity to explore. If they do not like their results, they have the power to turn failure into the reason they are motivated to try again. Recovering from failure is a valuable part of becoming aware, eligible, and prepared for life beyond our K-12 system. This is the time to remind them they control their effort and attitude, and no one else's.

High-leverage strategies like a project-based inquiry supports engagement, while being a positive example of culturally responsive teaching practices. When we provide choice for students, we open the door for them to bring in their culture, background, and experiences to the academic content we are providing. It not only helps them feel seen, heard, and valued, but it also helps as educators to be exposed to cultures different from our own. Most of us would not make a quick connection between social emotional learning and our science standards, but it is imperative we do. Modeling high expectations through the use of high-leverage strategies illustrates our belief in students. In turn, when our students feel our belief, they grow their trust and willingness to engage, no matter the situation. They feel a connection that allows them to know they are safe, even when feeling challenged, guarded, or uncomfortable. The development of self-management skills will also support their ability to communicate and listen to others' perspectives, as they work to become more socially aware, leading to a deeper understanding of others.

EDUCATOR SELF-MANAGEMENT JOURNAL REFLECTIONS

Once we have begun to gain self-awareness, we need to take action to move towards self-management. We can't think of a more valuable skill set to have that supports success in so many areas of our human experience. Managing emotions, getting organized, and persevering through obstacles is where the magic happens.

So get started responding to the following self-management prompts:

EDUCATOR SELF-MANAGEMENT JOURNAL REFLECTIONS

What are specific strategies you use to regulate big emotions, to return to baseline? Which ones could you also teach your students?

_____
_____
_____
_____
_____
_____
_____
_____

When considering the organization techniques above, are there specific ones you use to stay organized? Are there additional ones you have felt are helpful?

_____
_____
_____
_____
_____
_____
_____

What do you do when you are feeling unmotivated or stuck?

_____
_____
_____
_____
_____

Extend my thinking....

STANDING IN THE GAP FOR OUR STUDENTS!

SECTION 4

SOCIAL-AWARENESS

THE PUZZLE OF INSTRUCTION • 79

CASEL Definition of Social Awareness: The ability to understand the perspectives of and empathize with others, including those from diverse backgrounds, cultures, and contexts.

- Take others' perspectives
- Recognize strengths of others
- Empathy & compassion
- Understand & express gratitude
- Identify social norms, both just & unjust
- Awareness & appreciation of diversity

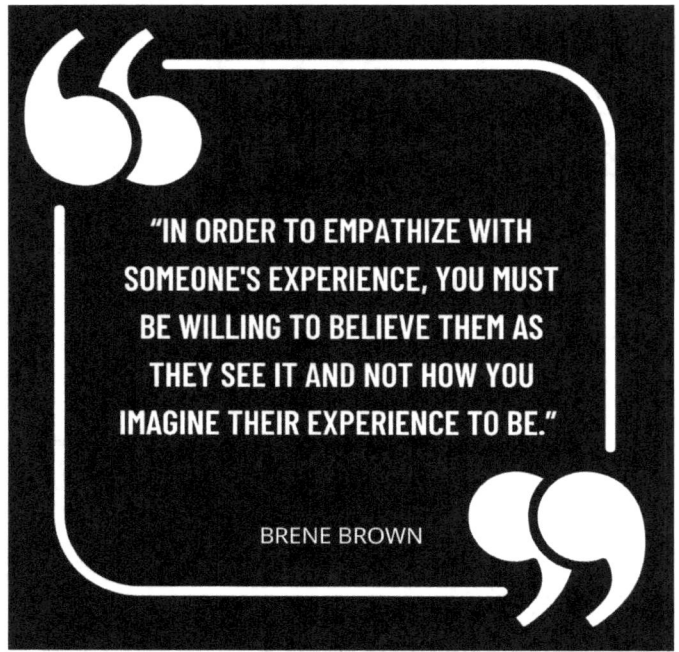

"IN ORDER TO EMPATHIZE WITH SOMEONE'S EXPERIENCE, YOU MUST BE WILLING TO BELIEVE THEM AS THEY SEE IT AND NOT HOW YOU IMAGINE THEIR EXPERIENCE TO BE."

BRENE BROWN

Social awareness is a skill we continue to work on throughout our lives. As educators, we often assume our students come to us with some abilities and strengths in this area. After all, aren't they highly motivated by peer relationships and social interactions? While some of our students enjoy being social, if social media is any indication, there are some big lagging skills around HOW to be socially aware. Anyone can post their thoughts online or speak about their opinions. However, true social awareness involves highly cognitive tasks, especially around perspective-taking and empathy.

The complex nature of social awareness became more evident to me (Kasia) when I had my oldest son. Around 4 years of age, we began to notice that something in his interactions with peers was different. Over the course of the next year, the plans and expectations we had around our lives quickly changed, when he was diagnosed with high-functioning autism. In his case, he struggles with smooth social interactions and often fails to understand others' perspectives or their theory of mind. The truth is, without explicit teaching of social awareness skills by his teachers, he would be lost in our educational system. This is true for many of our neurotypical students as well. Keeping their heads down, looking at their phones, and primarily interacting digitally during these politically divided times is not helping our students to thrive. It's up to us as educators to step up and integrate social awareness into our teaching.

GETTING ORGANIZED

As you consider the list of roles for both teachers and students in this section, you'll notice this is an extremely important, and content heavy area of social and emotional learning. Student development of empathy and ability to listen to other's perspectives with compassion, are skills being formed way before our kids set foot in our classrooms. You may even feel a bit overwhelmed to think about introducing social justice issues to your students, as you aren't completely confident they can apply these skills in a way that won't offend or cause harm to others. This is completely normal! It will take time to build a strong, collaborative, and supportive community. So where will you start? What is an access point you feel comfortable with for you and for your students? You don't have to do it all...... just do something and build from there. You and your students will figure it out, as you navigate the uncomfortable feelings of growth together.

Teacher Moves

Model and coach active listening through the use of talk moves and questioning strategies

Integrate multiple perspectives within lessons and student voices across content areas

Acknowledge the thoughts and feelings of students

Establish student identity-centered class norms and expectations collaboratively with students

Use diverse content and resources to represent all cultures and backgrounds across content areas

Encourage students to think flexibly

Student Moves

Actively listen to others' perspectives

Recognize strengths in others

Respond to others with compassion and empathy

Show concern for others and their feelings

Identify social norms

Understand social justice issues

Questioning prompts to integrate social awareness skills

① How are you an active listener?

② How do you listen and communicate with partners when you disagree?

③ Why is it valuable to listen to classmates with different thinking from your own?

④ What is your learner identity? How is it similar or different from your classmates?

⑤ What qualities do you bring to your group, and what qualities do you need from your classmates?

⑥ How do you help classmates when they are stuck?

BUILDING THE PUZZLE

Whether your students are 7 or 17, they love to focus on fairness. Or more specifically, unfairness. One guaranteed way to encourage student engagement is to provide relevant content focused on social justice issues. You may be apprehensive, thinking that could be a slippery slope. What about the parents? Won't they complain if I bring in a text or have a discussion that could be considered political? They might if you are the one leading the discussion and imposing your own views. That is not how we teach. Consider the following standard used in conjunction with a unit on the Civil Rights movement:

CCSS.ELA-LITERACY.RH.6-8.6: Identify aspects of a text that reveal an author's point of view or purpose (e.g., loaded language, inclusion, or avoidance of particular facts).

In this case, students are asked to analyze a text for clues to an author's purpose or opinion. In particular, focusing on the avoidance of facts or loaded language is a higher-level cognitive task to support their awareness. We LOVE to have our students look at historical documents or writings that were relevant during the time we are studying. In the case of studying the Civil Rights movement, students tend to become outraged with what they read and quickly come to a conclusion about the author's viewpoint. In addition, by providing visuals from the time, students are ready to discuss what they see and their feelings about the images. This leads to one of our favorite high-leverage strategies, which is essential to develop social awareness: Socratic Seminar.

Sounds fancy right? Well, the Socratic Seminar is a bit fancy. It's a student-led, formal discussion based on a stimulus like a text or picture. The important aspect is the student-led part. Students participate in this activity by creating critical thinking questions based on a topic, listening intently to peers, and sharing their thoughts and responses with others. It takes planning and practice, but over time, students gain a deeper understanding through collaborative dialogue and debate.

Most students know Jackie Robinson as the first Black Major League Baseball player. What they may not be aware of is his advocacy for the rights of Black Americans during the Civil Rights movement. Below, we have provided a copy of one of his letters to the President at the time, Dwight D. Eisenhower. In it, Robinson uses strong emotion to communicate the injustice of racism during the time. Providing a document with strong emotion helps students understand an author's point of view or purpose in a text.

Telephone
MUrray Hill 2-0500

425 LEXINGTON AVENUE
New York 17, N. Y.

THE WHITE HOUSE
MAY 14 11 36 AM '58
RECEIVED

May 13, 1958

The President
The White House
Washington, D. C.

My dear Mr. President:

I was sitting in the audience at the Summit Meeting of Negro Leaders yesterday when you said we must have patience. On hearing you say this, I felt like standing up and saying, "Oh no! Not again."

I respectfully remind you sir, that we have been the most patient of all people. When you said we must have self-respect, I wondered how we could have self-respect and remain patient considering the treatment accorded us through the years.

17 million Negroes cannot do as you suggest and wait for the hearts of men to change. We want to enjoy now the rights that we feel we are entitled to as Americans. This we cannot do unless we pursue aggressively goals which all other Americans achieved over 150 years ago.

As the chief executive of our nation, I respectfully suggest that you unwittingly crush the spirit of freedom in Negroes by constantly urging forbearance and give hope to those pro-segregation leaders like Governor Faubus who would take from us even those freedoms we now enjoy. Your own experience with Governor Faubus is proof enough that forbearance and not eventual integration is the goal the pro-segregation leaders seek.

In my view, an unequivocal statement backed up by action such as you demonstrated you could take last fall in deal-

MAY 26 1958

The President   Page 2   May 13, 1958

ing with Governor Faubus if it became necessary, would let it be known that America is determined to provide -- in the near future -- for Negroes -- the freedoms we are entitled to under the constitution.

Respectfully yours,

Jackie Robinson
Jackie Robinson

JR:cc

After reading the letter, students have the opportunity to analyze specific quotes and language from the text and to respond with their personal thoughts and reactions. This is done independently to prepare for the student-led discussion to come. This is a powerful activity to develop perspective taking, but remember, your classroom has to be a safe space for all kids for it to be successful. Since kids are reflecting independently, and then bringing those thoughts to the group, norms around respect are key. The last thing you want is for students to attack each other or leave the lesson feeling harmed and unheard. If you are looking for more strategies on how to best implement Socratic Seminars into your classroom lessons, a simple Google search will provide multiple resources. We have had students share that this is their favorite way to learn because they are so engaged with listening to and asking questions of each other.

Quotes/Language/Questions	Student Thoughts/Reaction: Socratic Brainstorm
What does Jackie Robinson mean when he says "I respectfully remind you, Sir, that we have been the most patient of all people."	
In paragraph 2, what does Jackie suggest when he says, "When you said we must have self-respect, I wondered how we could have self-respect and remained patient considering the treatment accorded us through the years"?	
Have "the hearts of men changed"?	
"As the chief executive of our nation, I respectfully suggest that you unwittingly crushed the spirit of freedom in negroes by constantly urging forbearance…." What does this mean to you? What does this represent to you?	
In Jackie's letter to the president, what line(s) do you feel is a directive to the president for taking action?	

If you consider the example student planning questions from AVID (Advancement Via Individual Determination) above, you can see how social awareness skills are essential to engage in this activity. Identifying the social norms around speaking up without interruption and appropriate speaking time are basics for engagement. Taking others' perspectives and responding with empathy and compassion are also higher-level social awareness skills developed in this activity. The use of accountable talking stems to keep the conversation respectful and also ensures multiple access points for students to engage in the conversation. Below, we've provided accountable talking stems to keep the conversation safe and supportive.

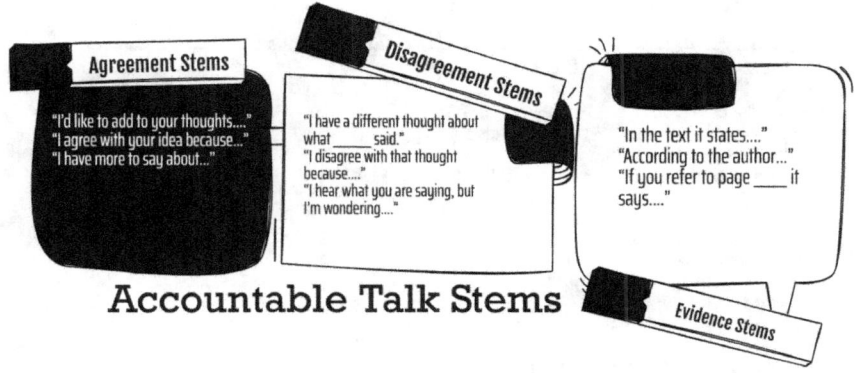

Example: Jackie Robinson's Letter to President Eisenhower (National archives: https://www.archives.gov/education/lessons/jackie-robinson/letter-1958.html)

SAMPLE SEL PLANNER FOR SOCIAL AWARENESS

Subject: Social Studies/ELA Integration   Unit: Civil Rights   Dates: 4 week project

Standard/Objective: CCSS.ELA-LITERACY.RH.6-8.6
Identify aspects of a text that reveal an author's point of view or purpose (e.g., loaded language, inclusion or avoidance of particular facts).

SEL Competency Focus: Working to understand perspectives and empathize with others including those from diverse backgrounds, cultures, and contexts.

SEL Objective: : I will work to understand the perspectives of others that differ from my own. I will look for similarities and differences and strive to put myself in their shoes.

Teacher Moves & Roles:	Student Moves & Roles:	Question and Prompts to Consider:
Model and coach active listening through the use of talk moves and questioning strategies	:Actively listen to other's perspectives Respond to others with compassion and empathy	How are you an active listener? How do you listen and communicate with partners when you disagree? Why is it valuable to listen to classmates with different thinking from your own?
Use diverse content and resources to represent all cultures and backgrounds across content areas	Understand social justice issues	
High=Leverage Task or Activity: Socratic Seminar		

Lesson Outline:
Opening: Review classroom norms and expectations for speaking and listening. Read Jackie Robinson's letter aloud.
Activity: Have students reread the letter (pairs/individually/small groups) and respond to questions and quotes on the Socratic Seminar brainstorm page. Review accountable talk and agreements for Socratic Seminars.

Reflection/Closing: Socratic Seminar

PLACING THE LAST PIECE

While there are many important aspects to social awareness, in our opinion, developing empathy and compassion for others is the highest priority. We tend to think about ensuring our students are critical thinkers who persevere through challenges, to be prepared for life beyond our educational system. While these qualities are important, they are basic skills that primarily focus on self. It's not through a focus on ourselves that we grow; it's through a focus on others. We can support this in our students through supporting their empathy lens.

Empathy is the skill of attempting to understand others' feelings, thoughts, and actions. To develop this skill, our students need to see others through a new lens or imagine themselves walking in their shoes. Instead of leaning towards judgment, they can move towards wondering about how someone might feel in a situation, or why they feel the way they do. How might their experiences have impacted them to feel or act as they are? True empathy happens when our students engage in curiosity, seeking to understand others and exposing themselves to different worldviews, leading to success in whichever college, career, or community pathway they choose.

For students, showing empathy for others can take many forms. As sixth-grade teachers, we've seen some amazing demonstrations of empathy by our kids. Whoever said middle school kids are only focused on themselves clearly doesn't know there is more than meets the eye when it comes to this age group. Empathy can look like a "cool" kid playing a game with "the kid" who has a difficult time making friends. Or, it could be seeing someone eating alone and choosing to invite them to sit at your table. Maybe it's noticing a kid who doesn't get any Valentine's grams and rushing to make sure they get one delivered the next day.

Empathy might look like not sharing a picture on social media because they wouldn't want that to happen to them. The point is, our students need to take the time to consider how someone else is feeling and do something to help them. As educators, the more opportunities we give our students to practice these essential social skills, the better prepared they will be when they leave us.

As we've grown, we've developed a deep appreciation of diversity and differences. For many educators, especially if you are white, you've had the privilege to grow up in an environment surrounded by people who look or think like you. Although this can be comforting at times, we are missing out on the essential experience of being different from those around us. You see, we grow as people when exposed to thoughts and experiences different from our own. The same is true for our students. How can they develop critical thinking skills and understand what they believe to be true in this world if they are only exposed to one worldview or way of life?

Kids need to listen to others and learn from their experiences, with eyes and hearts open. As they walk the halls at school, or interact with kids in classes, they should celebrate the differences they see. When their hearts are open, they will find that things like family norms are different all over. In these moments, they need educators walking alongside them. We need to encourage them to remember that just because something is different doesn't mean it's wrong. When faced with a person or idea different from their own, they can learn to fight feeling automatically defensive and lean into curiosity and a willingness to learn.

We once heard that the most powerful thing you can do is to stand up for a group of which you are not a part. In adolescence, with the desire to fit in, differences can become a source of conflict for kids and even lead to bullying. When our kids witness bullying or hear a racial slur, they have a moral obligation to stand up for others. It's through the development of social awareness skills, and a respect for diversity and differences, that this becomes possible. Students who leave us with the ability to grow and connect with others, rather than continue to support a divide, is exactly what our world needs to heal and flourish.

EDUCATOR SOCIAL AWARENESS JOURNAL REFLECTIONS

In our experience, listening to our students communicate their perspectives and grow in the areas of empathy and compassion is highly invigorating as an educator. Seeing the next generation asking questions of each other, stepping into another student's experience, and communicating their beliefs brings so much hope to us for our society. When was the last time you focused on this area in your personal growth?

Consider the following questions on the following page to continue your journey of social awareness:

EDUCATOR SOCIAL AWARENESS JOURNAL REFLECTIONS

Consider the group of colleagues you work with. Has there been a time when you felt disrespected or unheard? How did you react?

_____
_____
_____
_____
_____
_____
_____

How do you know what your students are feeling or experiencing when they walk into your classroom?

_____
_____
_____
_____
_____
_____
_____

Have you ever made an assumption about a student or family that turned out to be false? How did this affect your perspective going forward?

_____
_____
_____
_____
_____

Extend my thinking...

STANDING IN THE GAP FOR OUR STUDENTS!

SECTION 5

RELATIONSHIP SKILLS

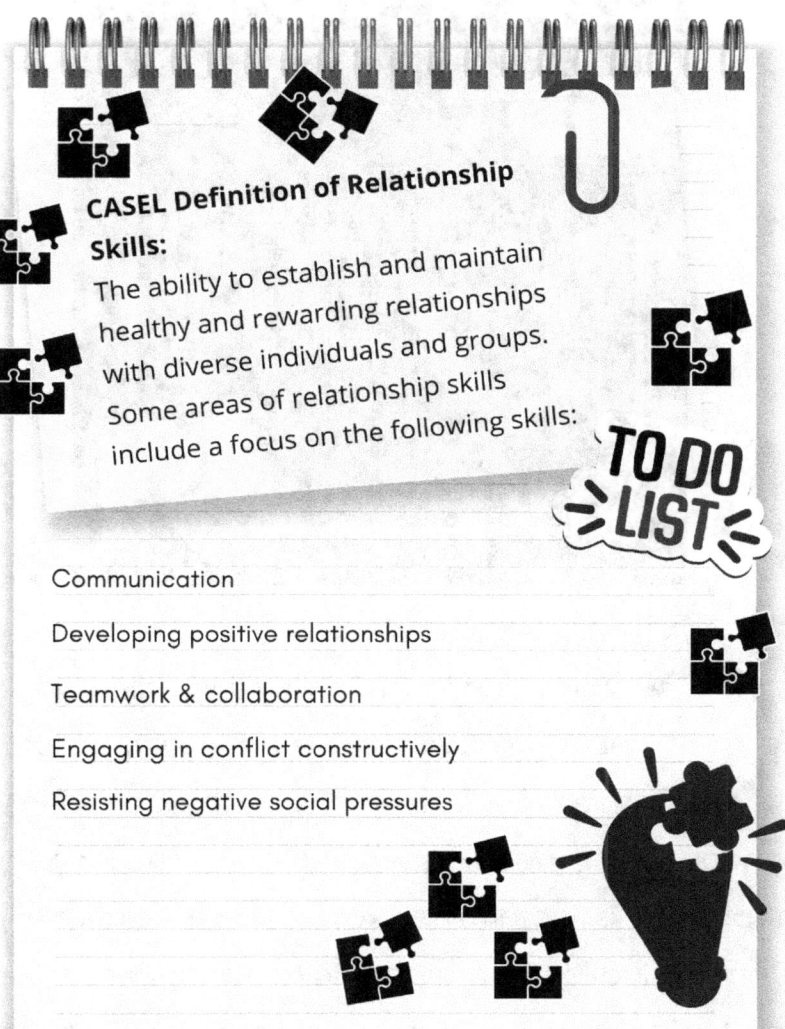

CASEL Definition of Relationship Skills:
The ability to establish and maintain healthy and rewarding relationships with diverse individuals and groups. Some areas of relationship skills include a focus on the following skills:

Communication

Developing positive relationships

Teamwork & collaboration

Engaging in conflict constructively

Resisting negative social pressures

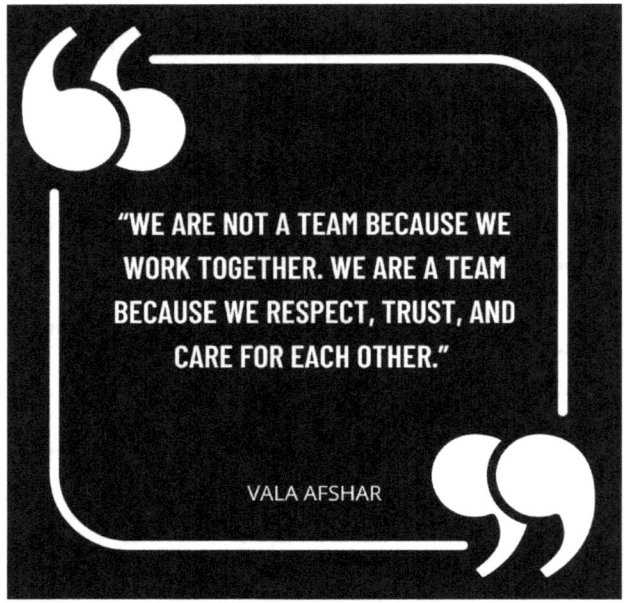

"WE ARE NOT A TEAM BECAUSE WE WORK TOGETHER. WE ARE A TEAM BECAUSE WE RESPECT, TRUST, AND CARE FOR EACH OTHER."

VALA AFSHAR

Communication is a key ingredient in the ability to form and keep healthy relationships. Success in the workplace and at school, becoming a leader, and achieving long-term happiness is determined by positive relationships. Communication can break down when our students are feeling peer pressure or struggling with self-management. When our students feel connected, they are not only invested in developing great communication skills, but they are also comfortable with being vulnerable and engaged in conversation.

GETTING ORGANIZED

We love this competency area of social emotional learning, and its heavy emphasis on healthy communication. For us, this is one of the areas we are most comfortable integrating across all content areas. Talking and sharing comes naturally to us, but this isn't the case for all educators or students. The thought of talking to another person, or in front of the class or group, can leave some people extremely uncomfortable. This is where the importance of integrating strong scaffolds is key. When facing a rush of body cues indicating fear and nervousness, attempting to find the right words or getting started can stop our kids in their tracks. So, when choosing a goal area for yourself and your students below, we always suggest adding frames, pictures, and scaffolds to support this area. Take that stressor off the table for your students and watch how they thrive.

Teacher Moves

Provide scaffolds and frames to support students' needs to encourage engagement in groups

Acknowledge conflict and resolution within content as well as model the thought process of conflict resolution

Provide opportunities for collaboration and conversation with differing viewpoints, including misconceptions in learning tasks and questioning strategies

Embrace the uniqueness of students, creating a sense of belonging to the classroom community

Engage students in discussions emphasizing important characteristics and qualities needed in healthy relationships

Student Moves

Communicate needs clearly to one another and teachers

Collaborate to problem-solve both social and academic tasks

Listen to others' ideas when working in a group; offer support to those in need; model upstander characteristics

Describe important qualities needed in friendships, and relationships, and apply them in the academic setting.

> **Questioning Prompts to Support Integration of Relationship Skills**
>
> → How do you let classmates know you care about/support them?
> → What makes a good team?
> → How do you handle struggles with yourself and with your classmates? What do you learn about yourself and others during those moments?
> → How did conflict impact your work time? How could it be prevented next time?
> → How was power and leadership distributed during your group work today? Whose voices were heard today and whose were not? Why? What adjustments need to be made?
> → How did you hold each other accountable to allow for 100% engagement and participation?

BUILDING THE PUZZLE

Mathematical discourse and collaboration are our jam! This is what drove a major shift in the delivery of our instruction. The people doing the talking are doing the learning, so we need to hear more from our students and less from us. The goal is to have our students build off of each other's ideas, to develop stronger academic connections and a willingness to seek support when needed. Taking the time to teach students how to ask questions and communicate academically and patiently with one another takes time.

We like to start with "Teacher Talk Moves." Having students re-voice what they heard the student before them say and asking students to add on to each other's thinking helps deepen the conversation, while keeping kids on track. Classroom agree and disagree hand signals provide all students the opportunity to be part of the conversation, even if they aren't quite ready to verbally speak up. Expecting students to share different strategies or thoughts in response to others is supported by having sentence starters and discussion frames explicitly taught and posted. With time, these scaffolds become a natural part of their daily discourse. The climate and culture of the room shift because questions become expected and therefore are celebrated. Also, participation and engagement increase because everyone has an access point to the conversation. What does this look like in action?

Standard 6.RP.A.1: Understand the concept of a ratio and use ratio language to describe a ratio relationship between two quantities. For example, "The ratio of wings to beaks in the bird house at the zoo was 2:1, because for every 2 wings there was 1 beak." "For every vote candidate A received, candidate C received nearly three votes."

Consider the following math task we provided for our 6th-grade students adapted from the College Preparatory Mathematics curriculum:

Comparing Rates Math Task

The 6th graders at Jackson School are raising money for their end-of-the-year activities. They need enough money to pay for the social DJ, pizza, soda, dessert, Subway lunch, bowling, etc. The student council has collected data about different kinds of fundraisers. They need your help with choosing a fundraiser activity.

With your team, discuss ways of comparing the fundraising strategies to be able to recommend which one to use. Use the data from the table and the questions below to start your discussion. Then write a note to the student council recommending which fundraising activity they should do. Be sure to justify your recommendation.

Fundraiser	Time	Expected Profit
Bake Sale	3 weeks	$500
Car Washes	4 weeks	$700
Recycling	⅗ week	$85
Yardwork	2 weeks	$320

How much will the class members earn if they spend 5 weeks doing car washes? How much will they earn if they spend 5 weeks doing yard work? Explain your reasoning!

How much money would the class earn if it recycled bottles and cans during the next three weeks of school?

The student council decided that the students will either sell cookies or hold car washes. They need help to compare the profit from cookie sales to the profit from car washes.

Teaching mathematical discourse is not an easy task for educators, but it is totally possible. AVID (Advancement Via Individual Determination) is a program that supports the shift of delivery of instruction to facilitation of learning through strategies encouraging engagement and access. A favorite AVID resource of ours is Costa's Levels of Questioning because it promotes higher level thinking and inquiry, while also providing students with the language needed to engage in discourse. When students are able to participate in conversations with teammates, they are building connections and relationships that support learning and growth.

The above math task is asking students to compare fundraising rates, and Costa's questions provide choices for students to participate depending on their level of understanding of the given task. We describe a level 1 question as a "Google it" question, meaning the answer is usually directly in the text or given information. A level 2, or "Noodle it," question takes a bit more brain power to respond. Students need to use the information provided in the problems, as well as think about and apply previous knowledge and understanding. Lastly, level 3 question, also known as a "Doodle it" question, requires processing both mentally and on paper. With regular use of Costa's questions, conversation and working relationships become an expectation for the climate and culture of the class.

Costa's Levels of Questioning can be used in a variety of ways. They can be the foundation for discourse while working in teams, or specific journal reflection questions for student responses. Eventually, when used frequently, students can use the format to independently create questions in any content area and bring them to group tasks or discourse opportunities. Here are some examples we have used with our students:

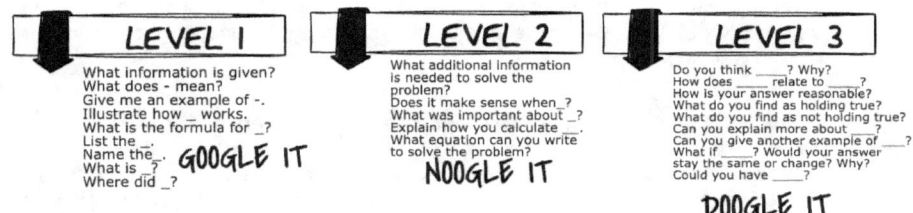

LEVEL 1
What information is given?
What does _ mean?
Give me an example of _.
Illustrate how _ works.
What is the formula for _?
List the _.
Name the _.
What is _?
Where did _?
GOOGLE IT

LEVEL 2
What additional information is needed to solve the problem?
Does it make sense when _?
What was important about _?
Explain how you calculate _.
What equation can you write to solve the problem?
NOOGLE IT

LEVEL 3
Do you think _? Why?
How does _ relate to _?
How is your answer reasonable?
What do you find as holding true?
What do you find as not holding true?
Can you explain more about _?
Can you give another example of _?
What if _? Would your answer stay the same or change? Why?
Could you have _?
DOOGLE IT

To ensure all teammates contribute and support each other in the learning process don't forget to support the conversation moving forward. "Who can add to what Kasia said?" What question do you have for Christa's reasoning?" Who can re-voice Kasia's thoughts in their own words?" These are powerful moves that encourage active listening while providing an opportunity to coach students to think beyond their own thinking. Learning to truly lean in and hear others supports their continued ability to understand perspectives that differ from their own.

SAMPLE SEL PLANNER FOR RELATIONSHIP SKILLS

Subject: Math   **Unit:** CPM Chapter 7   **Dates:** 2 days

Standard/Objective: Understanding ratio concepts and using ratio reasoning to solve problems.

SEL Competency Focus: Establishing and maintaining healthy relationships with diverse individuals and groups through communication, teamwork, and collaboration.

SEL Objective: I will ask questions, add on to others' thinking and listen to my math team to solve problems. I will value that team members may think differently than myself, and I will work to learn multiple strategies.

Teacher Moves & Roles:	Student Moves & Roles:	Questions to Consider:
Provide scaffolds and frames to support student needs to encourage engagement in groups	Collaborate to problem-solve social and academic tasks	How is your strategy similar to or different from your classmates? How were power and leadership distributed during your group work today? Whose voices were heard today and whose were not? Why? What adjustments need to be made? Can you add to (student name)'s thinking? Who can revoice what was just shared?
Provide opportunities for collaboration and conversation with differing viewpoints	Listens to others' ideas when working in a group	

High Leverage Task or Activity:
Supporting Student Discourse Through Levels of Questioning:

Lesson Outline:
Opening: Task connection to raising money for students' end-of-year celebrations and activities.
Activity: Fundraising task and group problem-solving. Review COSTA's levels of questioning to support continued discourse and deeper level thinking as a scaffold for communication.
Closing:
Student completion of a letter of recommendation for the end-of-year fundraising activity.

PLACING THE LAST PIECE

As humans, we crave connection and belonging. At the core of this need is our ability to establish and maintain healthy and fulfilling relationships. Healthy relationships aren't always with people who look the same, believe the same beliefs, or have similar backgrounds. Successful relationships require the necessary skills to connect with people different from one another. This is possible in our classrooms. We just need to provide the scaffolds needed for students to learn to work with all peers.

One way to develop strong relationship skills in the classroom among students is to intentionally model how to seek to understand individuals with differing views. This will not happen if we only group our students homogeneously. This can feel overwhelming and intimidating to some students. They have thoughts that sound like, "What if someone disagrees with me?" or "What if they disagree with me in front of others and I feel called out?" To be honest, this is hard for us as adults too. Learning and practicing how to share, explain, and question thinking in math will positively support their future conversations in other areas of their life.

Consider the world today and the events of the last few years. Many people feel more divided from others than ever before. It used to seem as though cooperative discussions and coming to a mutually beneficial decision were the main goals. Now, whether scrolling on social media or watching the news, when others feel differently about an issue or don't agree with our plans 100%, we assume they are wrong. We challenge you to make questioning and discourse a norm in your classroom. Encourage students to attempt to listen and understand others' perspectives in an effort to create connections and healthy relationships. (See a connection to Social Awareness here??) Fair warning: this is harder than it sounds. However, we wouldn't suggest anything we knew you weren't capable of. We encourage you to lead the change that empowers students to be accountable for their learning. These are essential life skills that students will be able to take with them on their career, college, or community pathways.

EDUCATOR RELATIONSHIP SKILLS JOURNAL REFLECTIONS

For some educators, you got into education to connect and support students. For others, it was a passion for a content area that led them to teaching. Whatever the initial motivation, strong relationships with our students and colleagues are essential for overall mindset and well-being. Who wants to spend the majority of their time in a building disconnected from others? While there are times you may feel you need a break so you shut the door to regroup, teaching in isolation will never lead to a feeling of fulfillment at work. Whether you consider yourself an introvert or an extrovert, connection with others is needed. This job is too hard and too important to attempt to do on your own.

Consider how you are doing in the area of relationship skills by using the questions on the following page.

EDUCATOR RELATIONSHIP SKILLS JOURNAL REFLECTIONS

How do my students and colleagues know I care about them? Do I feel like they care about me?

_____
_____
_____
_____
_____
_____
_____

What qualities do you appreciate in your teammates? What is missing or could be strengthened?

_____
_____
_____
_____
_____
_____
_____

Who is someone who has positively impacted your life and helped you to be who you are today?

_____
_____
_____
_____
_____

Extend my thinking...

STANDING IN THE GAP FOR OUR STUDENTS!

SECTION 6

DECISION-MAKING SKILLS

THE PUZZLE OF INSTRUCTION • 123

CASEL Definition of Responsible Decision-Making
The ability to make constructive choices about personal behavior and social interactions based on ethical standards, safety, and social norms.

- Curiosity & open-mindedness
- Identifying and analyzing problems & solutions
- Critical thinking
- Reflection & evaluation of consequences and impact of choices
- Reflecting on one's role and the well-being of self, family, and community

Our students are tasked with making responsible decisions regularly. As they are navigating the difference between fitting in and belonging, and the uncertainty of adolescence, they are constantly deciphering between what is fact and what is fiction. Providing them opportunities to evaluate and reflect on the cause and effect of decisions allows them time to develop their values and priorities as individuals. What a powerful opportunity we can provide our students. This reminds us of the quote from *Spiderman*: "With great power comes great responsibility." We get to coach and support our students as they work to distinguish what is most important to them and what will drive their moral compass.

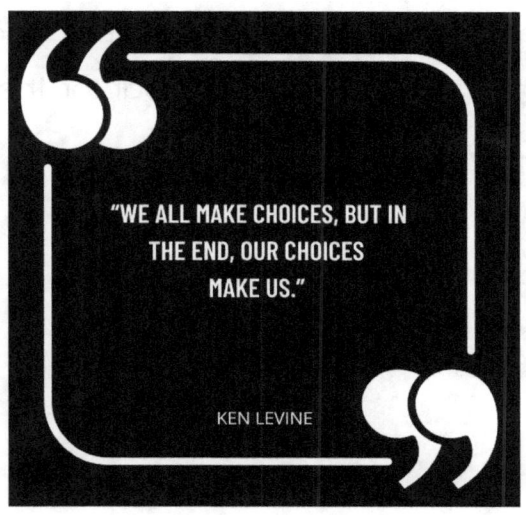

GETTING ORGANIZED

For much of the area of responsible decision-making, metacognition is needed. Metacognition is the ability to think about one's thinking. It's the process used to plan, monitor, and assess personal understanding and performance. Metacognition includes a critical awareness of thinking and learning as well as oneself as a thinker and learner. Looking at the list of roles and choosing one area will be difficult, as many overlap, and all are important. For us, working with 6th graders, we focus a lot on "Anticipate and reflect on consequences of actions (positive and negative)." This is where understanding and celebrating the identity of your students pays off. If you know them, and yourself, you will know how to make a goal for them as students, and you as their teacher.

Teacher Moves

Address conflict as part of a communication process; identify effective strategies for conflict resolution

Provide an opportunity to think, pair, and share consequences of actions

Engage students in discussions emphasizing possible outcomes to given scenarios/situations

Urge students to regularly evaluate and reflect on their decision making

Student Moves

Acknowledge problems and conflicts

Anticipate, and reflect on the consequences of actions (positive and negative)

Experience academic disequilibrium while stepping out of your comfort zone to meet goals

Take ownership in tough situations

Describe and model integrity

Questions to Integrate Responsible Decision Making

- How does the (character, historical figure, etc.) choices impact them and the people around them?
- Consider a conflict from group work time. What strategies could help the situation?
- How do your relationships with each other impact how you interact as a group?
- How can you use your strengths to make decisions? How do your decisions impact yourself and others?
- How did someone make a difference or impact you today?

BUILDING THE PUZZLE

The final piece of CASEL's competencies is centered around responsible decision-making. We all work on this in our classrooms daily. We encourage our students to think for themselves and to make decisions regularly, but what does that look like in instruction? We could talk to them each day about whether or not they did their homework or why they chose to not do it and the consequences until we are blue in the face. Does that really teach them how to work through the decision-making process? We want our students to be able to evaluate and reflect on the impact of their decisions. How does what they decide today impact their future self? I can visualize my (Christa) own daughter's eye roll as I ask her this question often. It is not always something our students want to discuss, but it is crucial to their success. Using text is a great way to evaluate the decision-making process while making it feel safe for students to engage in discussion around possible outcomes and dilemmas. In ELA class, use the following speaking and listening standard:

Comprehension and Collaboration:
CCSS.ELA-LITERACY.SL.7.1: Engage effectively in a range of collaborative discussions (one-on-one, in groups, and teacher-led) with diverse partners on grade 7 topics, texts, and issues, building on others' ideas and expressing their own clearly.

Students can analyze fictional characters in text to help alleviate vulnerability or discomfort that may occur when they feel their personal character is being analyzed. Using the story, students can engage in a discussion centered around the reasonings and thought processes behind the character's thinking, perspective, feelings, and decisions. Using evidence from the text, inferences, and their own experiences, they will be able to participate in deeper conversations and wonderings about alternative scenarios. With time and practice, a shared vocabulary, and community building, students will be able to empathize and connect to the character and imagine themselves in the character's situation. This creates an opportunity for students to connect their own decision-making and thinking process and the impact it has on themselves and others. We want our students to be able to evaluate the role of cause-and-effect in the decision-making process and understand the importance of reflection.

The opportunity to stop and reflect is an experience you don't want to miss with your students. They have made the t-charts about a problem and a solution. What now? They must take the time to evaluate how it went and think about people who were affected by the situation. This is crucial, as it helps them make responsible decisions in the future. Many times, our students, and we ourselves, make a decision and simply move on, happy to have any conflict or stress behind us. While this is common, those decisions can lead to experiencing even more discomfort or stress. How do we support our students when this happens? Using metacognition is a skill that allows students to practice visualizing and spending time with their thoughts. This is a tough skill as they have access to regular stimuli with technology devices, impacting their comfort level of their own thinking. Again, using a character from a text allows students to step back and practice evaluating and reflecting using decisions that do not expose them personally. So what does that look like in your classroom? In this example, we used the novel Ghost by Jayson Reynolds. We posed the following questions to our students:

Think about the consequences Ghost faces as a result of his decision to steal a pair of running shoes.

1. Do you think the way Coach punishes him is fair?
2. What would the consequences have been if Ghost had been stopped by the police instead?
3. What would the consequences have been if his mother had discovered the theft?
4. What would have happened if Ghost had never been caught?
5. Why might it have been better for him to get caught?

After consideration and discussion as a class, students take time to reflect and evaluate other possible solutions. Below is a graphic organizer we use with students as they process other options that may result in a positive or negative outcome:

Along with understanding the impact of decisions, students need to understand their perspective. For example, deep metacognition would require students to consider how they think; how their experiences impact their thinking; and who or what influences their thinking. This level of metacognition takes time and practice. Below is a clip of a digital chalk talk students used to analyze the perspective of Ghost's character.

- For me it means it don't mater where I live

- It makes him worry about telling people where he live because of the neighborhood he lives in

- Due to the fact that the neighborhood isn't the nicest place, I can see why people might judge him, but it doesn't give them a reason to stereotype Castle because of his past because it doesn't define him.

- Where I live. Where I live. When anyone ever ask about where I live, I get weird because people always treat you funny when they find out you stay in a certain type of neighborhood.

- He was being teased be Brandon Simmons back in pg34. He didn't like that.

- Agreed

- **How do his experiences impact his perspective?**

- After that awful night with his dad, now he looks at things differently.

- Why are they teased? Why is it not enough to be just him?

- I very much agree

- **How does that impact how he communicates with others?**

- I think it makes him more wary of telling people where he lives.

- Why?

- Maybe when ghost realized that everyone might make fun of the place he lived in his perspective changed.

- My heart feels heavy knowing that Castle is judged for where he lives. Our experiences and lives are part of who we are, but do not define who we are.

- Ghost's experiences impact his perspective because he was never really the same after that night with his dad, and also, because he lives in a certain kind of house, he is embarrassed

- He ran on the track and figured out that he wasn't just someone who wanted to race. He was fast, and he could be a racer if he wanted to.

- I agree

SAMPLE SEL PLANNER FOR RESPONSIBLE DECISION-MAKING

Subject: ELA Speaking & Listening

Unit: Ghost Novel Study

Dates: 4 weeks

Standard/Objective: CCSS.ELA-LITERACY.SL.7.1: Engage effectively in a range of collaborative discussions (one-on-one, in groups, and teacher-led) with diverse partners on grade 7 topics, texts, and issues, building on others' ideas and expressing their own clearly.

SEL Competency Focus: Making constructive choices about personal behavior and social interactions, based on ethical standards, safety, and social norms.

SEL Objective: I will evaluate and analyze Ghost's decision-making skills and how they impacts others and his future self.

Teacher Moves & Roles:	Student Moves & Roles:	Questions to Consider:
Provide opportunity to think, pair, and share consequences of actions Engage students in discussions emphasizing possible outcomes to given scenarios/situations Urge students to regularly evaluate and reflect on their decision making	Reflect on consequences of actions (positive and negative) Describe and model integrity	• How does the (character, historical figure, etc.) choices impact them and the people around them? • How can you use your strengths to make decisions? How do your decisions impact yourself and others?

High Leverage Task or Activity:
Metacognition

Lesson Outline:
Opening:
Identify a decision Ghost's character has made. Facilitate class discussion while modeling metacognition with question prompts.

Activity:
Student independent evaluation of character's decision and choices using the graphic organizer.
Using the same question prompts, create a chalk talk or jamboard for students to share their thinking.
Closing:
Have students read others' thoughts, ask questions, and build on each other's thinking.

PLACING THE LAST PIECE

Responsible decision-making is a crucial piece for our students' future success. They need opportunities to learn and to understand what personal, moral, and ethical responsibility is in a safe environment. Our current reality is driven by political decisions with varying opinions. They need time to learn and understand what they believe to be right and wrong. Also, they need to understand how they feel when other people have different ideas about what is right or wrong.

We would argue that we have a more balanced community when people have varying thoughts and perspectives. What will our students do if their perspective is different from others? Will they pause and listen, or will they "defend" themselves? Will it cause conflict? After listening to others, will they avoid or engage in stating their own beliefs? We want our students to be successful in making productive decisions for themselves while reflecting on all possible outcomes and impact. Our goal is for them to be okay with their own definition of morality and right versus wrong and to know others may not agree with them. Students can learn to be true to their beliefs, while attempting to see others' perspectives. Integrity, honesty, ability to evaluate information, analyze and solve complex problems, critical thinking and reasoning, and civic participation and engagement are just a few of the skills in high demand from employers. This is another way to help our students build the necessary skills needed to achieve their goals and career, college, and community ready. Taking time to build opportunities for students to experience responsible decision-making supports their ability to access viable pathways beyond their time with us.

Responsible decision-making opportunities also allow students to reflect through their own cultural lens. Using text and media to diligently work to reflect on their unconscious attitudes builds their cultural competency as decision makers—that is, understanding, sensitivity, and appreciation for the history, values, experiences, and lifestyles of others, as well as their own. Using relatable text and media also allows students to address and navigate real-world issues and decisions, asking themselves, "What does this material have to do with my life? Does this knowledge connect to an issue I care about? How can I use this information to take action?" We need to regularly assign activities, projects, and assessments that require learners to engage in metacognition, as well as identify and propose solutions to complex issues, including issues of bias and discrimination. Responsible decision-making allows our students to grow in integrity while knowing that what is best is not always easy.

EDUCATOR RESPONSIBLE DECISION-MAKING JOURNAL REFLECTIONS:

As educators, there are two frames of thought around students making their own decisions. On one end of the spectrum, there are educators who want to walk with and hold their students' hands through their decision-making process. On the other side of the spectrum, there are educators who have a "sink or swim" philosophy. Let them struggle and they will figure it out. Where do you fall on that spectrum? How can we find the balance between the two? For us, we have found that practicing thinking aloud about our decision-making process with students helps them evaluate and build their own skills. Asking questions to guide them as they are working, assists with processing their choices. Let's be there to walk alongside them when they "fall" or when things don't turn out as they had hoped. Being ready to coach and ask questions allows our students to productively reflect and evaluate their decisions for next time.

On the following pages are a few things to consider regarding your own practice:

EDUCATOR RESPONSIBLE DECISION-MAKING JOURNAL REFLECTIONS

When was the last time you considered the consequences of your decision before making it? How would you share this process with your students to support their metacognition?

_____
_____
_____
_____
_____
_____
_____

Does the material you provide for students connect to their own lives and interests?

_____
_____
_____
_____
_____
_____
_____

How easy is it for you to listen to your colleagues' perspectives and experiences when considering your decisions?

_____
_____
_____
_____
_____

Extend my thinking...

STANDING IN THE GAP FOR OUR STUDENTS!

SECTION 7

CONCLUSION

ADMIRING THE FINISHED PUZZLE

Social-emotional learning is not a new concept. In fact, it's been around since the 90s. It just seems to be on the radar of most educators these days. If we consider our journey as teachers, we've been truly focused on social-emotional learning concepts since the beginning. We didn't become teachers to teach content. Our "why" has always been supporting students through strong relationships, to further the healthy development of the whole child. Yes, we want our students to master academic skills like reading and writing. More importantly, we want to help them become positive, contributing members of society. From the beginning, we understood we are one piece of a big puzzle, helping students become who they are meant to be.

Pushback around social-emotional learning typically focuses on a couple of things: lack of time during the school day, and disagreement around who should be responsible for teaching these skills: teachers or families? We believe it's ALL our responsibility. We would love to think families are doing what they can to support these skills in their children, and positive relationships with coaches and mentors are available for all kids. However, with the rise in rates of depression and suicidal thoughts among teens, especially since the pandemic, we can't take anything for granted. This can't just be a home thing; it has to be a school and a community thing too.

We have a choice: we can be resentful of families perceived to not be pulling their weight around social-emotional learning, or we can assume they are doing what they can and step in to ensure we are filling the gaps for all kids. When you look at the data around the positive effects of teaching these skills and school achievement, including less negative peer interactions, increased problem-solving skills, and better impulse control, why do educators push back? If we are doing our jobs as educators, all learning can be considered social and emotional. It's not a box that we get to check each day; it's a teaching mindset. It is true that 20 minutes in an advisory class or 30 minutes in a morning meeting is not enough time to support growth in the social-emotional learning competencies. Through intention, we have to integrate student opportunities to practice these skills throughout the school day. This starts with helping students make connections between what they are thinking and doing, and the competency it connects to. For example, when a student shares they are becoming frustrated by a peer while working on a group project, they are practicing self-awareness while identifying emotions and their causes. When they share their concerns with their peer, they will use their skills around social awareness and relationship skills to address the problem and come to a solution. At first, they will not make these connections on their own, they will need us to help them.

While these skills help our schools and classrooms run smoother, development in these areas goes beyond their time with us in Pre K-12 education. Employers identify traits such as having a growth mindset, positive communication, adaptability, resilience, and empathy among the top desired qualities they look for in employees. In addition, colleges are less interested in perfect test scores and more focused on skills associated with social-emotional learning. On the Arizona State University admissions page, they identify 15 skills for college success. Among the 15, self-management, communication, collaboration, and critical thinking are identified as desirable traits. Where will our students learn these skills, if not practiced in our classrooms from a young age?

Brené Brown discusses hope in her book Atlas of the Heart. She shares that "hope is learned through relationships characterized by boundaries, consistency, and support." Brené also explains that hope is a way of thinking. We would argue that integrating social-emotional learning across all content areas within our schools will help our students to build hope. With hope, our students will set realistic goals. They will develop perseverance knowing they will need to have a plan A, B, and maybe even C to attain their goals. Alternative pathways will be part of their journey, and with hope, they will gain agency. They will believe they can achieve their goals and know there will be twists and turns, but they will seek support as needed.

The truth is, healthy social, emotional, and academic development is a right for all students. In public education, we take all students who come to us. We don't pick and choose. They come to us with different backgrounds, cultures, and experiences. It is our duty to ensure we provide a safe and healthy environment for them to thrive. This is supported by explicit teaching and integration of social emotional learning. When our students understand and apply skills in self-awareness, self-management, social awareness, relationship skills, and responsible decision making, barriers are removed, leading to success for all kids. Isn't this why we are in education? Don't we want to positively change the outcomes for kids? We can't do that if we are resentful and unwilling to move beyond the obstacles in our profession and if we can't keep our why at the forefront of our minds. Lack of time, testing requirements, and unsupportive parents and administrators will always be a part of our reality as educators. Our other reality is that every fall, we get a room, or rooms, full of students who are counting on us to help them be successful. They are begging for relationships and to be seen and valued for who they are. It's not about WHAT you teach; it's about HOW you teach. So be the change your kids need. Change your mindset from a "teacher of content" to a "teacher of humans," and truly impact your student's social, emotional, and academic development. This is how we can all stand in the gap for our students.

MEET THE AUTHORS

Kasia Gutierrez and Christa Pruss are a principal & student success coach team, dedicated to supporting educators with social-emotional learning integration. In addition to their 20+ years in education, most recently, the "Confidence Coaches for Kids" have spent the last several years focusing on the social and emotional needs of middle school-aged students. Their first published book for tweens and teens titled, "The Puzzle of You; Connecting Yourself a Piece at a Time During the Teen Years" offers reflection and journal opportunities encouraging students to become confident people of action. As educators dedicated to the belief it's possible to support students' needs without giving up instructional time, they provide conference presentations, including speaking at the Inaugural Summer SEL Institute at Harvard. In addition, working collaboratively with the South Carolina Department of Education, they have provided webinars and 10,000 book copies to South Carolina middle and high school students. Kasia and Christa look forward to supporting social-emotional learning for all educators and students throughout the country.

To learn more, visit www.confidencecoaches4kids.org.

www.ingramcontent.com/pod-product-compliance
Lightning Source LLC
Chambersburg PA
CBHW071851070526
44583CB00016B/1640